DISGUSTINGLY BEAUTIFUL

THE GOOD, THE BAD, THE UGLY OF COUPLES

DARYL L. FLETCHER SR.

A PANORAMIC GUIDE TO BETTER RELATIONSHIPS

After being married for 16 years, I went through a divorce. Toward the end of my marriage, I begin to chronicle my experiences of what worked and what didn't. Being single again was quite an experience and re-entering the dating lifestyle was very interesting as well. I compiled my experiences along with interviewing over 100 couples from first date to a couple that was married for 54 years. Through the interviews, the study of human behavior and my personal experiences. I've written...

"DISGUSTINGLY BEAUTIFUL"

Through my book, you can learn from my mistakes and the mistakes of others. You will read success stories of marriages that have stood the test of time and challenges. As a life coach, when I coach clients, I use a 3 legged stool approach to helping my clients. Life, Business and Relationships. If one leg is affected, the whole stool will be shaky. In the book I use concepts I learned from working in corporate America and certain business practices. I brought those concepts into relationships from a romantic standpoint. The world revolves around relationships and when we understand how relationships are designed to work, life can be more fulfilling. The way a door hangs in the doorframe is a relationship. The hinge holds the relationship together. Some hinges swing inward and some swing outward but if you don't understand the way the hinge swings the door won't open.

The book is broken down into pre-dating and dating and marriage concepts. I approached the delivery of the book in the following manner

What do they need to know?

Why do they need to know?

What do they need to do?

iii

Why do they need to do it?

What to do with challenges. And ways to solve challenges

If you have ever seen a couple that in love, it's always a beautiful thing. But after hanging around them with all their mushiness, affection and stuff, it can seem a little disgusting. Well that's the motivation behind the title. So enjoy this book. My prayer is that you find at least one principle that will help you have a Disgustingly Beautiful relationship.

Foreword For Distingustingly Beautiful

Over the last two decades, I have had the pleasure of working with and learning from some of the most amazing peak performers on the planet. People like Les Brown, regarded as the World's #1 Motivational Speaker, Dan Cathy, President and CEO of Chick-fil-A, James Malinchak, ABC's Secret Millionaire, Dolf De Ross, Real Estate Guru, Dr. Will Moreland, Leadership Life Trainer and so many more. I am always in pursuit of the next level of effective living through principles of productivity.

Throughout my years of devoted study on the topics of leadership, productivity, success, personal development, human behavior and performance strategies, I have learned that ACTION is the common denominator amongst high achievers. I mention this not to impress you, but to give you a glimpse into the journey that has brought you and I to this particular point in time. Life is about relationships; and the beauty of how we treat those relationships. You never know why people come into your life, nor do you know how your paths will cross in the future.

Twenty-five years ago, I met a young man by the name of Daryl Fletcher in Miami, Florida; and throughout the years, he has proven to be a man of action and integrity. He is the creator of the *1 Dynamic Life Coaching System*. Daryl has counseled over 50 couples towards better relationships; and experienced personal growth in his own relationship where he recently got engaged. He has spoken to over 5,000 people about life change principles. Daryl is a diligent student and was mentored by Coach Jeanne Mayo, Dr. Gloria Williams, Shawn McBride and Pastor Anthony E. Moore. He completed his first book and has seven in the pipeline. In his new book *Disgustingly Beautiful*, Daryl brings to light the principles behind the how and why successful relationships work. Most people want to have the benefits of a fairy tale relationship, but are not willing to put in the real work that it takes to make it a reality. The truth is, most people are walking in denial because they have an extremely detailed list of requirements that they are expecting to check off for their ideal mate.

Daryl releases his philosophy from a culmination of over 100 years of marital/relationship experiences into the mainstream so that people can learn, take advantage and be free in their own lives. The target audience: anyone, no matter where they may find themselves at in life, who desire a deeper and more fulfilling understanding of how relationships work. It's simply a "heart grabbing and minding blowing" book in terms of relational understanding and a perpetual growth mentality.

Daryl Fletcher has masterfully captured the principles in a panoramic guide to better relationships. If you are serious about taking your relationship to the next level, despite how long you have been in a relationship, the teachings in this book, if taken to heart and acted upon, will propel you to immediate improvement or what I like to call Evidence and Result (ER).

Dr. Vernet A. Joseph
America's #1 P³ Speaker & Strategist
Best Selling Author
www.livetoproduce.com

Chapter Summary

PRE-DATING CONCEPTS

1. **You're the plan I never thought of** - Being open to Possibilities for a new relationship.

2. **Definite Maybe** - What is the potential of the relationship and the person that you are seeking to be with?

3. **Inquire and require** - Are you asking the right questions from your potential mate? Are you requiring what you expect?

4. **The Void is Over** - Are you really ready for a new relationship?

5. **Would you date You** - If it were possible, would you date you?

6. **Inventory** - What do you actually possess and bring to a relationship?

7. **Beyond the Body** - How important is physical appearance in a relationship?

DATING CONCEPTS

1. **They Judge me, they judge is not (There goes the judge)** - Creating a non-judgment zone for your relationship.

2. **Freedom over Fear** - Fear is an emotion and emotions are indicators not dictators.

3. **What's it worth** - People invest in so many things and place value on so many things rather than what's important in life.

4. **The Fight before the Fight** - You fight for the relationship everyday before challenging times appear.

5. **Deliberate love** - Love is an emotion however emotions are indicators not solely dictators.

6. **Beyond the Body**
   a. Their body may begin to change but you love shouldn't fade.

7. **No Plan B** - The moment you have an option is the moment you have the tendency to take an option. Focus and commitment

8. **Audio Technician** - There are always 4 conversations going on in a relationship
   i. What is said
   ii. What is meant
   iii. What is heard
   iv. What is felt
   The art of communication is to get all 4 of those on the same page

POST DATING/MARRIAGE CONCEPTS

1. **Maintenance is cheaper than repairs** - Rather than waiting for to repair a relationship maintain it

2. **Your greatest asset is each other** - Investing in each other has a great return.

3. **What's Next – Movement vs. Monument** - Don't get stuck in your past experiences and moments of celebrations.

4. **What's the mission** - Why are you together? What's the purpose of your union?

5. **There is no room automatic** - Nothing will always come easy, there are certain things in a relationship that you will have to work for.

6. **The Long Walk Home** - Men are microwaves women are crockpots. Intimacy is a long walk home.

7. **Beyond the Body** – Soul & Character vs. Body

8. **Building a Bridge (Conflict resolution)**
    a. Compartmentalize
    b. Commitment
    c. Communication

Table of Contents

Section 1: Me, Myself and I

Section 2: Highway of Dating

Section 3: Marriage what's it all about?

Section 1:
Me, Myself and I

Chapter 1

You're the plan I never thought of...

What you pursue is determined by what you value

Many people dream about their future spouse from when they are young. Maybe they have a certain choice of eye color, height, skin tone or hair color, body type, etc. It's easy to imagine what they may look like, but other characteristics become more important as you grow older. However, as a relationship evolves, many factors become a higher priority rather than what a person looks like. Relationships are filled with endless possibilities and this can be scary at times, but we are typically drawn to a certain type of person when looking for a life-long companion. Athletes may be drawn to athletes and it's common for people working together either for the same organization or within the same profession to end up dating or even married because of obvious similarities.

People like what they like and there is nothing wrong with that, but what is your like based on? Is it only about how attractive they are? Is it solely based on their physical appearance? Are you looking for some eye candy? Or for someone to just look good on your arm? "Arm Charm."

Being open to possibilities in a relationship is vital. Possibilities present opportunities for the unknown and the unforeseen to happen. When you are open to possibilities, you open yourself up to a world and things that you might not have thought of or experienced. People often talk about what could possibly go wrong, but let's switch our thinking to what could possible to go right. Your future relationship is a possibility. Don't limit your happiness or fulfillment in a relationship by a physical package or just how attractive someone is.

During the holiday season in a particular year, I remember standing in line waiting to get some gifts wrapped. As I stood in line, I remember admiring the beautiful samples of the gift-wrapping they placed on the wall. I remember how well put together the packages were. Nicely wrapped, looking perfect. The unique thing about those gifts was that they had

3

nothing inside them. They were empty. From the outside, they looked good, but would bring no one happiness if you were to give them to someone. They were just for show. They brought nothing to the table but a pretty outside.

Beauty can be said as skin deep. But what's underneath that skin is the real question and the real value. A person can come in a nice package but what is on the inside? You may be drawn to a

Physical attraction is just that. It's an attraction. It attracts but it doesn't keep.

particular type of physical package when looking or expecting a mate but, what about a person's character and moral and value system on the inside?

If you're looking to get into a relationship, you may have your eye on someone. You may be observing this person as a potential partner. They may have all the assets you like from a physical standpoint but what about what's inside. Are they attractive on the outside like the gift samples I saw on the wall but empty on the inside? Do they possess character, values and morals that will last in the long run? Physical attraction is just that. It's an attraction. It attracts but it doesn't keep.

The person you think you desire to be with may have the right physical package but do they have the right heart package is the greater question.

If you are currently single, there may be a person in your life right now that you have been overlooking because they don't seem to meet the desirable physical or visual package you have been expecting. Maybe they aren't physically what you dreamed of. Nonetheless, perhaps this individual treats you lovingly and respectfully and as such communicating to your exact need in ways you have never been loved and treated before. It's easy to fall into the trap of dating the person who seems to have life all put together – nice car, house, dream job – but how would that person treat you? Are they too busy in the mirror checking themselves out rather than telling you how good you look or how significant you are in their life or how much they mean to you? Are they selfish and only concerned with what they have going on?

Having been a pastor for over six years, I have heard countless stories of men and women from all backgrounds meeting under unbelievable circumstances. Over the course of time and in writing this book, I would pick the brains of couples that had been together for a long time and ask certain questions. Such as:

What attracted you to this person?

Why did you stay with this person?

Over and over, I have heard stories of couples that were drawn together and stayed together, thanks to their partner's values. It was what was inside that person that made them stay. One thing may have attracted them, but it was another thing that helped them stay together, another thing kept them bonded.

Values vs. Desire

Desire is simply something you want and it can be based on something good or bad for you. It's often shaped by your surroundings and circumstances in life, such as wanting coffee or a greasy meal after working hard all day. You may want a vacation to warmer weather in the middle of winter. You may suddenly want a new pair of sneakers when your friends come strolling in with new shoes. Not all desires are bad, but basing a relationship strictly on desire can end in disaster.

Values are what shape and mold you and what you can't live without. You may value good and bad things, but these are more long-term. This could be acceptance, adventure, assurance, balance, and belonging, helping others, working hard, career, commitment, encouragement, family, community, involvement, learning, marriage, trust and a long list of various other attributes. Your values may change over time, but you will not be satisfied with someone long-term if they don't share many of the same values.

Here are a few questions to ponder as you think about how your values and desires have shaped the way you have approached relationships in the past.

Selah Moment

Am I looking for a mate based on my values or desires?

What will I value in a mate 10 years from now?

What are some of the selfish qualities people in previous relationships have shown?

Who in my life have I been overlooking?

Would I be open to the possibilities of finding love in an unexpected place?

What are my values?

What are my desires?

Dr. Larry Alan Nadig, PhD Clinical Psychologist, suggests that similar core values are highly crucial in selecting a mate and vital in order to maintain an effective relationship. These include:

Morals

Religious preferences

Spiritual views

Cultural views

Political views

Each of these core values plays a vital part when looking for that special someone who may potentially become your life-long partner. There will be plenty challenges and issues that arise over time which you cannot possibly predict. You can, however, predict how a person will respond to certain situations based on their values. When tough times in a relationship come, (and they will come) how your partner responds will be drawn up in their value system, not their physical appearance. How will they respond; will their looks help your relationship or will their values help your relationship? Remember the gift wrapping I talked about earlier? Let's imagine that I brought some beautifully wrapped gifts home for Christmas. I told everyone that the packages have some great gifts inside, the gifts on the inside would help them when they were in trouble or when they had a serious need, but they could not open the gifts until they really needed to. So the persons I gave the gifts to carried these packages around just to show everyone they

8

had gotten something. They were pretty much just showing them off. They took pride in the packages because they were pretty, they were big, and they were the envy of everyone that looked at them. These packages were there just for eye candy, so that the people with them could be envied.

The time came when the individuals with the packages needed them. They experienced a challenging time. So the persons with the gift went to open the package because they had an expectation that what they valued and what they needed would be in the gift but they quickly found out that there was nothing of any value in the packages. Now the person is presented with disappointment and frustration. This happens far too often in relationships built on superficial desires of carnal attraction. You may have even experienced it yourself.

A minister traveled to a church to speak and became a repeat guest. He took notice of a unique lady and began to inquire about her. He found out that the young lady was indeed single and she was quite impressive. This young minister asked the lead pastor of the church to arrange a meeting. The lead pastor agreed. At the meeting, this traveling minister expressed his interest in this particular lady. He said to her that he was interested in courting her and that she was very attractive, intelligent and it would be an honor to pursue a relationship with her. The young lady allowed the minister to finish his presentation of his interest. Upon his completion and expression of his intentions, the young lady informed him that she had no interest in him whatsoever. She indicated that this man was not her type at all. She liked taller, more physically impressive men. She was used to dating more attractive men. The traveling minister was short and slightly round. The lead pastor interrupted the meeting and began counseling them. Now, I don't know all the details of everything the pastor said, however, I do know that he talked about being available to possibilities. Rather than just looking at the outward appearance of this traveling preacher, he asked the young woman to look at his heart. His heart was pure, honest and his intentions were respectable. This young lady agreed to go on at least one date with the traveling minister.

Upon looking beyond this minister's external features, she found that their values, vision and what they were looking for in a mate were very similar. She looked at this man through her value system rather than just a checklist of shallow desires and external looks.

The couple later married and began traveling and speaking together and they have been married for over 10 years. They are compatible in unprecedented ways that wouldn't have been possible with other people.

A person's value system will determine whether they stand by you when you are sick and during a challenging financial time, not whether they are tall or short, have a volleyball player physique or could lose a few pounds. It's a person's values that will stick with you when your future children are challenging. Choosing a mate who has a similar value system as you will help you grow stronger, have a happier relationship full of respect and love.

Pursue your mate based on values and not just looks and selfish desires

What if the person who would treat you in the manner you wanted and needed to be treated came in an unexpected package? What if that person would love you the way you wanted to be loved and wasn't physically the way you always dreamed about – or was lacking the outward appearance you desired? People often choose a mate based on superficial desires or merely based on physical attraction. It's worthy to be physically attracted to the

11

person you engage in a relationship, but the issue with solely focusing on this is that physical appearances change over the course of months and years. Look at an elderly couple – their relationship is based on more than physical features. They may have learned that, what is really essential about a person is what is on the inside. Styles and fads come and go and your interests will also change. But what a person values will stick with them for life and it is an expression of their, moral standard and fortitude to get through life's twists and turns. You need more than a pretty face as a partner to walk through good and bad times in life. You need more than just "eye candy" or an "arm charm". Would the person you have your sights on now stand firmly by your side if you were in a car accident and expected a prolonged recovery in the hospital? Would they work hard to provide for you and future children? Would they drop everything to help a family member in need without building resentment?

Ask yourself this question and demand an honest answer: has a relationship worked out as expected in the past when I selected a potential partner solely based on physical attraction?

Have you ever stopped to consider what values are most important to you in a relationship? Your values should be higher and greater than your desires. It takes time to work this out, but who you decide to spend time with will change as you determine what you truly value. The person that is really for you may be the plan that you never thought of...

Chapter 2

Definite Maybe

You don't get what you wish for; you get what you work for.

In 1955, a man walked into a small restaurant that had been serving burgers, fries, shakes and sodas. The man was very impressed with the success of this small establishment and saw that this restaurant had the potential to be something great. He was stunned by the effectiveness of its operation. Their ability to produce quality products was amazing. He talked to the owners of the restaurant and pitched his idea that would take this restaurant to the next level. He pitched the idea of franchising this small restaurant and making restaurants like it all over the country. To accomplish this, he persuaded both franchises and suppliers to buy into his vision. He communicated that they would be working with the restaurant and not for the restaurant. He desired to make a partnership. That man's philosophy was to be in business for yourself, but not by yourself. His philosophy was based on a simple principle of a 3-legged stool. Franchises, suppliers, and employees. The stool was only as strong as the 3 legs it stood on. That man was Ray Kroc, the restaurant was McDonalds. They formed a partnership that most people across this country and even the world has had an opportunity to take advantage of. The partnership was birthed out of the potential of what could be accomplished when the 2 parties came together.

Every person has potential, but the question is: potential for what? Potential has been defined as, "capable of being or becoming." So, when you are looking for a potential mate, what kind of potential are you looking for in a person? You have potential. The person you end up in a relationship with has potential. Selecting a potential mate means you are choosing a road map in life that will lead you down a path. This path will have limitations within the confines of the relationship, but how this comes together depends on your potential and that of the other individual.

When selecting a mate, you guys have the potential to do something, but what is that something. Essentially, you guys are creating a partnership. In an article on Inc.com the questions was asked, what makes a good business partnership? In the article, they listed 3 principles that made for great partnerships.

1. Integrity
2. Work Ethic
3. Vision & Goals

Finding the right business partner can make or break a business and finding the right life partner has the potential to make or break your life. Transferring these same principles from the business world into a relationship, we are going to look at how these principles can play a part in selecting a mate.

A partner is someone who will be with you through all of life's challenges. They stay close during the storms and help you fully celebrate your accomplishments. In the story of Ray Kroc and the McDonald brothers, both parties knew that there were challenging times that would happen and they would share in the successes and failures of the organization. When you're single, all of your successes and failures fall on you, but going into a potential relationship, things will start

Are you looking for a partner or are you looking for perfection?

16

to be split (ideally) down the middle and shared. Let's answer a real question.

Are you looking for a partner or are you looking for perfection?

We often look for that perfect mate that has it all together. They have the perfect job, they have the perfect family and upbringing, they have the perfect car, house, they would never say anything inappropriate to us, blah, blah, blah, etc. and so one...

Let's be honest, perfection doesn't exist.

Rather than looking for perfection, let's try to focus on seeking out a partner.

Partnership verses Perfection

> *Let's be honest, perfection doesn't exist.*

Relationships are the perfect examples of partnership, but often people seek perfection over accepting a person for who they really are. This is troublesome because both parties in a partnership are encouraged to dream, have separate responsibilities, listen

17

respectfully to one another and enjoy freedom. Everyone comes into a relationship with what I'll refer to as baggage that disrupts the idea of perfection.

Remember the childhood favorite story The Wizard of OZ? Now there was a group of people that had baggage. Dorothy had issues at home, the lion was a coward, the Tin Man didn't have a heart, and the Scarecrow didn't have a brain. What a rag tag bunch of people. The main story line of the movie was that these 4 people were on the yellow brick road to see the Wizard of Oz. The Wizard was going to help them with all their issues and help Dorothy get back home. While on their journey to see the Wizard, they encountered challenge after challenge. This group of people had apparent issues and obvious baggage, but they worked together as partners in order to accomplish a goal. Their imperfections and baggage were put on the back burner, because what was more important was they needed each other for the journey ahead. Where one partner lacked, the other partner made up for it. In actuality, their imperfections brought them closer and gave them an opportunity to learn from each other and build a partnership.

When we seek out a mate that is perfect, we limit ourselves and cause ourselves frustration because no one is perfect.

We all are human and will make mistakes along the way and have baggage. Don't let a great potential mate get away because they didn't fit your ideal state of perfection. Just because you are stronger in one area of your life, your potential partner may be weak in that exact area; don't totally rule them out.

Here are some questions I want you to ponder:

Selah Moment

- What did you learn from your parent's marriage (or lack of marriage) growing up?
- What baggage are you bringing into a relationship?
- What areas do you see yourself as imperfect?
- What are your potential partner's strengths and weaknesses?
- What are your strengths and weaknesses?
- What do you see yourself as being responsible for?
- What do you see your potential partner being responsible for?

Remember that you have a past too as you think through these questions. What strengths are you drawn to versus what areas do you dislike? Seek out the person's heart, because this is more important than creating a checklist of what they have done right and wrong in your eyes. We all make mistakes, but what matters the most is realizing that life is full of processes. Does the person give up on a friendship they should fight for? Do they try to control the actions of another person? Are they striving to gain a new perspective in a difficult situation? Paying attention to how another person processes these situations – whether bad or good – will give you insight into how they may grow as a person. Remember, everyone has potential and the outcome of a situation is not always as important as how they deal with it. Going through life, you will experience injustice, unfair treatment and dishonesty. Does the person you are considering as a potential mate share the same perspectives as you? Are your hearts connected on what matters the most? Have you determined what is most important to you?

Remember those 3 key elements of a great business partnership. Let's unpack them and talk about them a little more.

Integrity

In the business world, integrity can mean either loss or gain of valuable resources, money and time. Taking this same principle and transferring it into a relationship, integrity can pay major dividends in the longevity of your potential relationship.

Integrity could be defined as doing the right thing when no one is looking. Once again, we are all human and no one person is perfect but past patterns are a good indicator to predict future performance.

Paying attention to a person's conversation about their previous relationships can paint a picture of what they have a pattern of doing. Do you and your potential mate choose to do what's right all the time? This doesn't need to be a checklist of right and wrong, but you can probably gather a general sense of whether they tend to cut corners or go the

> *past patterns are a good indicator to predict future performance.*

extra mile. Your potential partner doesn't have to go back inside a store to pay for something they forgot was in the cart, but integrity says they do it anyway. Integrity says you don't believe what appears to be gossip and you don't spread it. Talk about preventing unwanted drama! Integrity says you will return money to someone who dropped it when you could have pocketed it. Integrity means you pay your taxes, pay back money you borrowed and return belongings that are not yours. This is critical to maintain trust in a relationship, so take a hard, long look at whether

21

your potential relationship includes integrity. Integrity ensures you are considerate of others and striving to honor what is right. Lack of integrity will take you

People will show you who they really are if you pay attention. When people show you who they are, believe them. The life they live speaks louder than the words they say.

down a path that is destructive in the long run, although it may not seem like a big deal in the moment. Lack of integrity is one of those things that can come back and bite you. If you have someone that is trying to get into a relationship with you when they are already in a relationship, what do you think that person will do if you two were to get into a relationship? I know we all like to think the people we meet treat us different and we are special and the sun rises and sets on our smile, but that's not the case.

People will show you who they really are if you pay attention. When people show you who they are, believe them. The life they live speaks louder than the words they say.

Selah Moment

- Do you sense that integrity has a place in your potential relationship?

- Will you try to do the right thing all the time?
- Will your actions match up with what you claim?
- Do the actions of your potential partner match up with what they claim?
- Is there room to identify that you have made a mistake and to confess?

Work Ethic

In the story of Ray Kroc and the McDonald Brothers, one thing that Ray Kroc admired about the brothers was that they were very effective in their restaurant. This effectiveness came from a tremendous work ethic. Ray knew that with his work ethic and their work ethic, it would be a great partnership to accomplish something awesome. He was drawn to them because they shared similar work ethics. Think about your work ethic. It's easy to assume your potential partner will work hard, but this is not the reality that many people experience. Do you want someone who sits around playing video games and waiting for life to just happen, or someone who is willing to work for what they have? This plays out in many ways, including how they value and appreciate what they own. If they complain about their situation and aren't trying to rectify it, they may have the idea that they deserve possessions, vacations, vehicles, etc. to be given to them. This sense of entitlement divides many couples because there is a lack of appreciation for the one who is working hard and earning what they have. In a relationship, you don't want to feel like you're the only one working in the relationship. If you put in 100%, you want your partner to put in 100%. In order for a relationship to grow, it's vital that work ethic be a key factor. The old saying says "a chain is only as strong as its weakest link". A relationship is only 2 links, so make sure your potential mate has a similar work ethic in order to build a strong bond.

Selah Moment:

- Do you have a strong work ethic?
- Do you try to work as many hours as possible?
- Would you rather someone else pay your way?
- Does your potential mate choose to work more or relax more?
- Does your potential mate set financial goals he/she work to meet?
- Do you sense a good balance between how much you work and how much your mate works?

Vision and Goals

Diana Ross had a popular song in the 70's with the lyrics "Do you know where you are going to, do you like the things that life is showing you?" That's a good question. Many of us have a path that we are on and want to continue with that path. We have plans and things we would like to accomplish. You may already be set in a specific lifestyle and that's not bad – it's normal as life goes on. It's easy to dream about things like vacations, traveling the world, volunteering, having a big house, being involved in plays and musicals, and running a marathon. Dreams are what keep you going and help you set goals. Your lifestyle is created around what you do, who you hang out with and even what you choose as your career. What about your potential partner? Do, they have dreams, desires and even a few pieces of their lifestyle determined.

Listen intently to your potential mate – whether you think you have met him/her or will in the future. Do their dreams match up with yours? Can you dream together? Can you envision life with this person as your partner to strive toward a lifestyle you can embrace? Understand that events happen in life that can drastically change your lifestyle. You can't control a cancer diagnosis, how you will feel when and if kids come into the picture, an unexpected pregnancy after already having two children, how life will change after a parent dies. Continue to dream and focus on the lifestyle you would love to have, but leave margin for change and the unexpected to captivate you and your future partner. We can't predict the future but having like minds can help your vision and goals in the relationship. Similar goals and visions serve as a road map to where you want to go. If an unexpected circumstance or event takes you off course, you can still come back to where you left off with the right road map. You and your partner should share similar visions and goals. Plenty will happen over the course of time that will try to distract you from your relationship, but going in the same direction can help elevate some of the friction along the way.

Life is full of twist and turns and unforeseen situations. Viewing your relationship as a partnership is critical because it allows you to give your mate space to navigate. They have margin to explore the hobbies and interests they enjoyed before you two came together. Demanding they change to fit your idea of perfection is controlling who they are. Choosing to make changes together is how you work together in this partnership. Every relationship has potential; potential to accomplish something great together or the potential to ruin someone's life. The potential to do something great together lies in the ability to select a partner that shares similar goals and visions. We are not all perfect, but we all have potential. That potential is a definite maybe...

Chapter 3

Inquire and require

He who asks questions cannot avoid the answers.

I used to work for a telecommunications company while I was in college. While I was there, I excelled and was promoted to a team supervisor for this company. I was young, full of energy and ideas but had no idea on how to properly hire people. The interesting thing about that was that most of my supervisor peers, some much older than I, had the same experience in hiring people. Sometimes it seemed like we were hiring anyone and everyone that came in the door. If you had a pulse, an ID and a SSN you were hired. I say that jokingly, however, that's what it felt some days. Our turnover rate was crazy. We would hire 40 people and maybe 15 would make it to their 1 year anniversary. We had an actual revolving door situation going on. It was a noticeable dilemma and many of my peers saw what I saw but didn't have much motivation to stop the cycle of the revolving door. More than just lack of motivation, it was more of not knowing what to do about the problem. It was like sitting a 7th grade math student in front a calculus book and asking him to solve an equation, but the 7th grader hasn't even taken Algebra 1 yet. Any company I was ever involved with, I always had a desire to make the company better somehow. Even at a young age, this company wasn't any different. I went to my director at a time and asked him, his views on our turnover rate. We shared the same views that something had to be done about what was going on. However, he lacked the 'know how' as well. We exchanged ideas and communication that day, however, I walked away from that meeting thinking, that nothing wasn't going to change. A few weeks later, I received an email from the office of the director. The subject title read "Mandatory Training." I opened that email and it was a training on "How to hire the right Candidate for the Job." Looked like my conversation didn't fall on deaf ears. The day of the training came and I was excited about what was about to take place. I had no idea what to expect, I just knew that it looked like we were going to make some changes around the company as a whole. Over the course of the training, we as a company and a group of ill prepared managers and supervisors didn't know what we were doing in the hiring of people. We had the "warm body" syndrome. Where we just hired people just to say we had somebody, rather than hiring the right quality person for the job. One of the most important factors of that training was that I found out we were asking the wrong questions in the interviewing process. The following are samples of the type of questions we would ask:

- Do you like computers?
- Do you like talking with people?
- Are you reliable?
- Are you punctual?
- Do you like working with people?
- Are you a team player?

All these questions were relevant to the positions we were hiring for, however, that told us nothing about the person's previous working pattern or the character and personality of the person we wanted to hire. These questions required yes or no answers. It didn't give us an indebt look at what type of employee we were potentially hiring. It just told us that they knew how to say yes or no and also how to talk. In the interviewing process, we wanted to create dialogue and get a sense of what each person was actually bringing to the table. After taking the training, here was how those questions went:

- Tell me about a time you had to work with computers?

- Describe a time you had to use you communications skills to overcome a problem?

- Tell me about a time on your previous job that they solely relied on you?

- Tell me about a time that you had to be on time, but was running late; how did you handle that issue?

- Describe your last experience in working in a group environment?

- Talk to me about a time you had to work in a team? What was your experience? What were your challenges, if any? How did you overcome those challenges?

The questions after the training required us to dig a little deeper with our questioning. We had to talk a little bit more but it also created a dialogue and conversation with the applicants. This gave us a better opportunity to evaluate the potential and possibility of the applicant and painted a clearer picture of what they brought to the table. As a result, our turnover rate went down and we were able to hire more quality people rather than just warm bodies.

Now let's take this same principle to the dating world. How many times have you gotten involved with someone and found out that they were not the person you thought they were? You guys went out on a date, talked about your favorite foods, or favorite movies; you talked about things but you didn't get to the meat of the person. You knew nothing about their character but you liked their personality. You just met their representative that they were bringing to the table so they would be on their best behavior. I know it may take time to really get to know a person but sometimes when we meet a person that we potentially want to date, we also don't ask the right questions to even understand if that person is worth investing or spending any of our time. In this chapter, we will go over some typical questions that one may ask when you first met someone. We will then go over those questions and make sure that we are asking them in an open-ended manner and not just asking closed-ended questions. Before we get into those questions, I want to talk about Character vs. Personality.

Character can be defined as a pattern of qualities of a person that are distinctive from other persons that make up that individual's personality. Character traits are both good and bad. We all have a certain level of character, typically a person's moral beliefs contribute to their character.

Personality can also be defined as a set of qualities that are distinct to a person, which makes him unique as an individual. The difference is that personality is commonly associated with outer appearance and behavior of person and is usually learned or developed while character is deep-rooted and a part of the inherited make up of an individual. Let's look at some differences between character and personality.

- If you sit at a meal and without fail, your potential partner reaches out his/her hand to bless or pray over the food. – That's Character
- When you go to a party and your partner is outgoing and the life of the party. They really know how to keep that party going – That's Personality
- Your potential partner respects your choice of celibacy and does not try to push or persuade you to change your views – That's Character
- Your potential partner is confident at work and loves to be in control. They run the show and like to be in charge to make sure things go right – That's Personality

Here are some positive character attributes:

- Honesty
- Respect
- Compassion
- Punctual
- Loyalty
- Fair
- Maturity
- Apologetic
- Attentive

Here are some negative character attributes

- Demanding
- Selfish
- Jealous
- Loving
- Disrespectful
- Careless
- Inconsiderate
- Stingy
- Impatient

Positive Personality Traits

- Optimistic
- Charming
- Confident
- Suave
- Persistent
- Valiant
- Exuberant
- Trusting

Negative Personality Traits

- Laziness
- Picky
- Finicky
- Sneaky
- Self-Centered
- Impulsive
- Cowardly
- Malicious

At the end of the day, character can be summed up as what has been instilled in you based on values. And personality can be what you appear to be.

Character is who you are; personality is who you want people to believe you are

Let's not get fooled on how we perceive people's personalities and think it's their character.

Let's take a look at how we ask questions when we first meet someone. What we ask is not as important as how we ask it. How you ask a question will either create dialogue or just give someone the opportunity to tell

Character is who you are; personality is who you want people to believe you are.

you what you want to hear. Remember we are discerning their character and their personality. Here are some typical first date or getting to know you questions.

- Do you have a good relationship with your parents?
- Do you have a good relationship with your ex?
- Are you ready for a relationship?
- Do you like kids?
- Are you romantic?

- Do you like to go to church?
- Do you like going out on dates?

Look at the questions we've listed. These are typical questions people may ask when they are getting to know someone. These questions are closed-ended questions and only allow the person answering the questions to give a yes or no answer. Let's be honest; have you ever found yourself asking questions like this and then later found out that the person was not upfront with you? Have you ever asked any of these same questions? Let's see how we can ask the same questions to create a different type of response. We are requiring more information from our conversation and creating dialogue to discern what type of person we may be really dealing with.

- Tell me about the relationship you have with your parents?
- When was your last relationship? How long did it last? Why did it end?
- Describe your ideal relationship; is that what you are looking for right now?

- How is your relationship with your kids? (If they don't have kids) What is the relationship with any kids that may be in your life? I.e. Nieces, nephews, family members, etc.
- Describe your ideal date?
- Tell me about your moral beliefs and what makes up you belief system?
- What is your idea of a great date?

I have listed here a few ways to ask open-ended questions to give you an idea of how to create dialogue when getting to know someone. In addition to these 7 questions, at the end of this chapter, I have listed more thought provoking questions. At the end of the day, you can't receive what you don't request. You won't know what you don't inquire. Asking the right questions in the right way can open up a great dialogue and paint a better picture about a person's personality and their character.

Here are some more sample questions to create a dialogue with someone that you are interested in getting to know:

- What's your current passion in life?
- Who is the person you admire the most and why?

- Describe your philosophy on personal debt?
- How did you choose the career that you are in?
- What is your idea of a committed relationship?
- What is your greatest regret?
- What are 3 goals you have for the next 12 months?
- What is most important in a relationship to you?
- What was the last book you read? What was the greatest take away from that book?
- What is one thing you would like to change about yourself?
- What is your most embarrassing moment?
- How do you handle anger?
- What do you do to relax?
- How do you think men and women love differently
- Do you think relationship counseling works and why or why not?
- Are you parents still together?
- Define love?

Chapter 4

The Void is over

Your past does not define you, it prepares you.

When I looked up the word void, I was amazed at what I got.
Though I had an idea of what the word meant but for
clarity's sake, I had to look it up. Void can be described as
the following:

- An empty space
- A gap or opening
- Something experienced as loss

With that being said, what are we talking about in this
chapter? We are taking about voids. People often times
medicate themselves with a variety of things, some people
call them vices. I remember when I first moved to Atlanta
years ago, I went to a party that some of my co-workers were
having. At this party, I quickly noticed that there were a lot
things going on that I was not used to and that I did not
normally participate in. There was smoking going on, and

not just cigarettes. There was an excessive amount of alcohol being consumed. A young lady came up to me and asked me if I wanted anything to drink; I declined her offer. She then asked if I wanted to smoke anything; I also declined that offer as well. Her next statement to me was "Then what's your vice?" I looked at her and said I didn't have one or maybe I did but I just didn't know what my vice was at the time.

Vice used as preposition would be defined as "Instead of" or "In the place of." People have vices that they are addicted to but don't even realize that these things are addictions. They have things that they do to medicate themselves from the problems of the world. They want to detach themselves and void themselves of any feelings or emotions. Rather than dealing and addressing the issue at hand, they attached themselves to a vice. They feel that the vice now helps them cope but the challenge or issues are still there. All the vice does is exchange one problem for another. "Instead of" dealing with the issue, they are now entangled in a relationship with a vice that will not help them nor will it make things any better. Some common vices are drugs, alcohol, working, shopping, eating, the list could go on and on. But one vice people often overlook is the vice of other people. Replacing one person with another. When relationships end, sometimes we have a tendency to try to want to find a replacement a little too quickly. This is found more often in the males. Now don't get me wrong, females do it too and I will address that in a second but let me talk to the males first.

Males have a tendency to have a "warm body syndrome." The warm body syndrome is when you try to replace someone for

Feelings are not facts; feelings are indicators not dictators. but it doesn't keep.

someone else however you are not really interested in the replacement you're really just trying to get over the hurt of the last person. This type of situation rarely ends well. Most people just end up getting hurt, used and abused; and it's usually the replacement, aka "the rebound" The reason is because the male was just trying to fill a void. He may have been used to having someone around and doesn't want to be alone with his thoughts or feelings so instead of dealing with them, he will find someone to use and distract him from his feelings. We have become a society where our feelings have taken over what we say and do. Feelings are not facts; feelings are indicators not dictators. However, we have allowed our feelings to dictate to us what we say and do, rather than dealing with the real issue at hand. When relationship ends, there may be feelings of hurt, betrayal, abandonment, lost, failure etc. These feelings may be real however, they don't give us a reason to act out a certain way that is not beneficial. They may end up hurting someone else in the process. If you're hurt, that gives you no excuse to hurt someone else. If you have been betrayed, you shouldn't do things that will betray others. If you feel abandoned, lost or failure; finding someone new too quickly just to masks those feelings is not helpful. You have just added more to your life to handle and more unresolved issues to deal with later on down the line.

Ladies, you are not let off the hook. It has become more popular for women to have the warm body syndrome. However with women, it plays out a little differently. The female species can be a very emotional creature. Most decisions come from an emotional place. After a break up, they may have a tendency to blame themselves and question their self-worth resulting in being very critical of themselves. After a break up, you may ask yourself the question, "Well what's wrong with me?" There is no need to question who you are, it's just that particular relationship didn't work out. Just because there is an attraction between two people doesn't make it an automatic love connection. Just because you guys had common interest doesn't mean you guys were meant to be life partners. Relationships can end for a number of reasons. Just remember to learn from your experiences and find ways to be better and not bitter. If you dated someone and there was something they didn't appreciate about you, don't be so quick to seek out someone that finds that one thing about you more alluring. You have now started trying to fill the void of validation with accommodation. Validation comes from within. No man can validate who and what you are. You are creating a vice for yourself and trying to fill a void with something that doesn't belong there.

When I was in kindergarten, we would have this activity. The activity was where you would take a peg shaped object and place it in a hole that matched the object. If it were a square peg then it would belong in the square hole. If it were the round peg than it would belong in the round hole. If it were the star peg, it would belong in the star hole, and so on; you get the idea.... There were many sets for all the children and many times the sets would get mixed up. That meant that the pegs and holes were all different sizes and we would have a variety of options for our pegs to fit in. We had small, medium and large pegs and holes. The objective was to get the perfect match but it was hard sometimes because things got so mixed up. So what would happen, you would have square pegs in round holes and round pegs in square holes and the children would have thought they did a good job because they fit. In reality, they fit but they didn't belong

43

there. They fit because maybe the square peg was smaller so it could squeeze in, but it didn't really belong there. It wasn't the right size but it filled the space. That's what we do sometimes when we enter a relationship prematurely with someone just to fill a void. They fill the space or void but they weren't designed for that spot or really don't belong. They are just taking up space in our lives and time is a precious gift that we should not waste. So the question becomes; "what do I do after a break up to make sure I've dealt with my feelings and I'm not just trying to fill a void?" I call it the 4G system. You can begin to apply these 4G's in an effort to assist you in making sure you're not just trying to fill a void.

Grieve - The grieving process can be a funny process. It will look different for each individual however here are some stages of the grief process
- Reflection of the entire relationship
- Admittance to your part in why the relationship may have failed. What part if any did you play in the demise of the relationship?

Give – Give yourself time to heal

Grow – What did you learn from the situation, take account of things that took place in the relationship. What worked? What didn't work?

Groom – Take honest inventory of yourself. Are you ready for a relationship? Are you in a good place? Are you groomed to be with someone?

Chapter 5

Would you date you?

Making bad decisions is a part of life; blaming others for your bad decisions is immature.

I've heard many single women and men say, "I'm dating myself." The question here is, "what does that mean?" Is that taking yourself out on a date? Is it siting at a restaurant alone by yourself? Is it walking with yourself in the park? These things are essential parts of a date but not necessarily dating or courting someone for a relationship.

What do I mean by that?

Are you properly assessing your ability to get along with others and your personality?

In 2012, I was introduced to an assessment system called Myers Briggs Assessment. The Myers Briggs Type Indicator assessment is a psychometric questionnaire designed to

46

measure psychological preferences in how people perceive the world and how they make decisions. Perceptions and decision making play a major part in a relationship. It goes back to the old saying, "is the glass half empty or is the glass half full?" The decisions you have made in your life have been influenced by your perceptions and how you see the world. I once heard a quote by Dr. Samuel Chand, President of Beulah Heights College; He said, "life is the sum of where you been and who you have been with." I would like to add something to that as well, "Life is the sum of where you been, who you been with and the information you have received." Now what does this have to do with dating yourself, or answering the question would you date you? We will get to that in a minute but I want to unpack your perceptions and your decision making. Let's talk about this Myers Briggs stuff for a second.

Now there are several personality test out there. I have taken a few, however, I would say that I discovered a lot about myself talking the Myers Briggs. I want to give a brief breakdown on how it works and how it affected me.

The Myers Briggs Type Indicator was created by Katharine Cook Briggs and Isabel Briggs Myers. The indicator was based on an extrapolation from the typological theories proposed by Carl Gustav Jung's 1921 book Psychological

Types. Jung introduced a theory which said that there are 4 principal psychological functions by which human experience the world. Jung's type theory introduced a sequence of four cognitive functions (thinking, feeling, sensation, and intuition). Each having one of two orientations (extraversion or introversion), for a total of eight dominant functions. The Myers–Briggs theory is based on these eight functions, although with some differences in expression. From these eight functions, we have a total of 16 different personality types. Now we won't have time to go over all of the personality types but we will review some personality traits and definitions and expressions of these personality types.

Attitudes: extraversion/introversion

The Myers–Briggs assessment uses the terms extraversion and introversion Extraversion means "outward-turning" and introversion means "inward-turning". These specific definitions vary somewhat from the popular usage of the words. Note that extraversion is the spelling used in MBTI publications.
The preferences for extraversion and introversion are often called "attitudes". Briggs and Myers recognized that each of

the cognitive functions can operate in the external world of behavior, action, people, and things ("extraverted attitude") or the internal world of ideas and reflection ("introverted attitude").

People who prefer extraversion draw energy from action: they tend to act, then reflect, then act further. If they are inactive, their motivation tends to decline. To rebuild their energy, extraverts need breaks from time spent in reflection. Conversely, those who prefer introversion "expend" energy through action. They prefer to reflect, then act, then reflect again. To rebuild their energy, introverts need quiet time alone, away from activity.

Functions: sensing/intuition and thinking/feeling

- Two perceiving functions: sensation (usually called "sensing") and intuition
- Two judging functions: thinking and feeling

Each person uses one of these four functions more dominantly and proficiently than the other three; however, all four functions are used at different times depending on the circumstances.

Sensing and intuition are the information-gathering (perceiving) functions. They describe how new information

is understood and interpreted. Individuals who prefer
sensing are more likely to trust information that is in the
present, tangible, and concrete: that is, information that can
be understood by the five senses. They tend to distrust
guesses, which seem to come "out of nowhere". They prefer
to look for details and facts. For them, the meaning is in the
data or information they have.

On the other hand, those who prefer intuition tend to trust
information that is less dependent upon the senses, which
can be associated with other information (either
remembered or discovered by seeking a wider context or
pattern). They may be more interested in upcoming
potential. For them, the meaning is in the underlying theory
and principles which are manifested in the data.
Thinking and feeling are the decision-making (judging)
functions. The thinking and feeling functions are both used
to make rational decisions, based on the data received from
their information-gathering functions (sensing or intuition).
Those who prefer thinking tend to decide things from a more
detached standpoint, measuring the decision by what seems
reasonable, logical, causal, consistent, and matching a given
set of rules. Those who prefer feeling tend to come to
decisions by associating or empathizing with the situation,
looking at it 'from the inside' and weighing the situation to

achieve, on balance, the greatest harmony, consensus and fit, considering the needs of the people involved. Thinkers usually have trouble interacting with people who are inconsistent or illogical, and tend to give very direct feedback to others. They are concerned with the truth and view it as more important.

Lifestyle preferences: judging/perception

Myers and Briggs added another dimension to Jung's typological model by identifying that people also have a preference for using either the *judging* function (thinking or feeling) or their *perceiving* function (sensing or intuition) when relating to the outside world (extraversion).

Myers and Briggs held that types with a preference for *judging* show the world their preferred judging function (thinking or feeling). So TJ types tend to appear to the world as logical and FJ types as empathetic. According to Myers, judging types like to "have matters settled".

Those types who prefer *perception* show the world their preferred perceiving function (sensing or intuition). So SP types tend to appear to the world as concrete and NP types as abstract. According to Myers, perceptive types prefer to "keep decisions open".

For extroverts, the J or P indicates their *dominant* function; for introverts, the J or P indicates their *auxiliary* function.

Introverts tend to show their dominant function outwardly only in matters "important to their inner worlds". For example:

Because the ENTJ type is extroverted, the J indicates that the *dominant* function is the preferred judging function (extroverted thinking). The ENTJ type introverts the auxiliary perceiving function (introverted intuition). The tertiary function is sensing and the inferior function is introverted feeling.

Because the INTJ type is introverted, however, the J instead indicates that the *auxiliary* function is the preferred judging function (extraverted thinking). The INTJ type introverts the dominant perceiving function (introverted intuition). The tertiary function is feeling and the inferior function is extraverted sensing.

So what does all this have to do with dating yourself and relationships?

I encourage you to take the test if you have never taken it; you can find it online. Look at the information from the assessment and try to begin to rediscover who you are and how you see the world. There is also information as to what personality types work well together. Here is a list and brief description of the all Myers Briggs personality types.

ISTJ

Quiet, serious, earn success by thoroughness and dependability. Practical, matter-of-fact, realistic, and responsible. Decide logically what should be done and work toward it steadily, regardless of distractions. Take pleasure in making everything orderly and organized - their work, their home, their life. Value traditions and loyalty.

ISFJ

Quiet, friendly, responsible, and conscientious. Committed and steady in meeting their obligations. Thorough, painstaking, and accurate. Loyal, considerate, notice and remember specifics about people who are important to them, concerned with how others feel. Strive to create an orderly and harmonious environment at work and at home.

INFJ

Seek meaning and connection in ideas, relationships, and material possessions. Want to understand what motivates people and are insightful about others. Conscientious and committed to their firm values. Develop a clear vision about how best to serve the common good. Organized and decisive in implementing their vision.

INTJ

Have original minds and great drive for implementing their ideas and achieving their goals. Quickly see patterns in external events and develop long-range explanatory perspectives. When committed, organize a job and carry it through. Skeptical and independent, have high standards of competence and performance - for themselves and others.

ISTP

Tolerant and flexible, quiet observers until a problem appears, then act quickly to find workable solutions. Analyze what makes things work and readily get through large amounts of data to isolate the core of practical problems. Interested in cause and effect, organize facts using logical principles, value efficiency.

ISFP

Quiet, friendly, sensitive, and kind. Enjoy the present moment, what's going on around them. Like to have their own space and to work within their own time frame. Loyal and committed to their values and to people who are important to them. Dislike disagreements and conflicts, do not force their opinions or values on others.

INFP

Idealistic, loyal to their values and to people who are important to them. Want an external life that is congruent with their values. Curious, quick to see possibilities, can be catalysts for implementing ideas. Seek to understand people and to help them fulfill their potential. Adaptable, flexible, and accepting unless a value is threatened.

INTP

Seek to develop logical explanations for everything that interests them. Theoretical and abstract, interested more in ideas than in social interaction. Quiet, contained, flexible, and adaptable. Have unusual ability to focus in depth to solve problems in their area of interest. Skeptical, sometimes critical, always analytical.

ESTP

Flexible and tolerant, they take a pragmatic approach focused on immediate results. Theories and conceptual explanations bore them - they want to act energetically to solve the problem. Focus on the here-and-now, spontaneous, enjoy each moment that they can be active with others. Enjoy material comforts and style. Learn best through doing.

ESFP
Outgoing, friendly, and accepting. Exuberant lovers of life, people, and material comforts. Enjoy working with others to make things happen. Bring common sense and a realistic approach to their work, and make work fun. Flexible and spontaneous, adapt readily to new people and environments. Learn best by trying a new skill with other people.

ENFP
Warmly enthusiastic and imaginative. See life as full of possibilities. Make connections between events and information very quickly, and confidently proceed based on the patterns they see. Want a lot of affirmation from others, and readily give appreciation and support. Spontaneous and flexible, often rely on their ability to improvise and their verbal fluency.

ENTP
Quick, ingenious, stimulating, alert, and outspoken. Resourceful in solving new and challenging problems. Adept at generating conceptual possibilities and then analyzing them strategically. Good at reading other people. Bored by routine, will seldom do the same thing the same way, apt to turn to one new interest after another.

ESTJ

Practical, realistic, matter-of-fact. Decisive, quickly move to implement decisions. Organize projects and people to get things done, focus on getting results in the most efficient way possible. Take care of routine details. Have a clear set of logical standards, systematically follow them and want others to also. Forceful in implementing their plans.

ESFJ

Warmhearted, conscientious, and cooperative. Want harmony in their environment, work with determination to establish it. Like to work with others to complete tasks accurately and on time. Loyal, follow through even in small matters. Notice what others need in their day-by-day lives and try to provide it. Want to be appreciated for who they are and for what they contribute.

ENFJ

Warm, empathetic, responsive, and responsible. Highly attuned to the emotions, needs, and motivations of others. Find potential in everyone, want to help others fulfill their potential. May act as catalysts for individual and group growth. Loyal, responsive to praise and criticism. Sociable, facilitate others in a group, and provide inspiring leadership.

ENTJ

Frank, decisive, assume leadership readily. Quickly see illogical and inefficient procedures and policies, develop and implement comprehensive systems to solve organizational problems. Enjoy long-term planning and goal setting. Usually well informed, well read, enjoy expanding their knowledge and passing it on to others. Forceful in presenting their ideas.

Now in order to properly use this information to your advantage, taking the assessment is key. I learned so much about myself when I did it. I used that information to help me interact with people that were in my life and it really helped.

Personalities are major when it comes to relationships. I find that personalities should do 2 things; Connect and compliment. Fundamentally, when seeking a mate you are building a team. A team must work and play well together in order to win. Each person on a team has a role and the team members must know and understand their role. Each team member should connect to the other team members and compliment them. If connection and complimenting are not a part of the team then the team will eventually fall apart and not accomplish whatever the goal is for the team. Ask any general manager or coach that has built a great championship team. Connection and complimenting are not an easy task to complete but when mastered, it creates an environment where the team wins when it counts.

Your personality should connect and compliment your partners. Think of it this way. Let's say that men are screws and women are nuts. A screw has its function of tightening things by screwing into it and a nut has its function of holding things together by connecting to the screw. The screw and nut are different in their design, shape and function but together they connect and complement each other. When you take the right size screw and connect it to the matching size nut, they build a bond that compliments each other's differences. They are not the same but when connected properly, they will work well together and accomplish the goal of keeping whatever they are attached to together.

Oftentimes in relationships, we try to find people that are just like us. We want somebody that would do what we want them to do, or handle an issue the way we want them to handle it, or clean how we would clean etc. What is the point of dating someone that is exactly like you? Really, think about it...... If you put 2 screws together, can they accomplish anything? If you use only nuts on a job of fixing things, will you really hold anything together? I have seen in several relationships where people spend so much time trying to make their partner just like them. Trying to find ways where they can change their partner. In a relationship, you are not there to change your partner, you are there to connect and complement them. You are different for a reason. We spent a lot of time in the beginning of this chapter talking about the Myers Briggs Personality Type Indicator. Discovering more about yourself will assist you in knowing whom you connect better with. It will also show what personalities you compliment and what personalities compliment you.

You need to know how you interact with other people because you may think and be a great catch but not everyone that catches you compliments you.

The title of this chapter is "would you date you". Well, most people would say that they would date themselves. It's easy to go out on a date alone or "date yourself" but that's not the point of the relationship. A relationship involves more than just you, it involves other people. You need to know how you interact with other people because you may think and be a great catch but not everyone that catches you compliments you

Stop spending your time trying to change the people you meet or the partner you may have. You guys are different for a reason. Learn to complement each other and not change each other. Don't date you, date your compliment.

Daryl L. Fletcher Sr.

Connect - With each other
Compliment – Each other
Commit – To each other
Continue – With each other

Chapter 6

Taking Inventory?

It's difficult to appreciate the value of others when your own self-assessment is over valued

A **SWOT analysis** is a structured planning method used to evaluate the **strengths, weaknesses, opportunities and threats** involved in a project or in a business venture. I learned of SWOT while working in corporate America. I was a supervisor in a telecom company. We were constantly trying to evolve as a company and make our corporation a better place to work and provide a great product to our customer. Often times we would use SWOT to know what steps we needed to take in order to accomplish goals and projects that we had coming up.

A SWOT evaluation can be carried out for a product, place, industry or person. It involves specifying the objective of the business venture or project and identifying the internal and external factors that are favorable and unfavorable to achieve that objective(s). Some authors credit SWOT to Albert Humphrey, who led a convention at the Stanford Research Institute (now SRI International) in the 1960s and 1970s using data from Fortune 500 companies. However, Humphrey himself does not claim the creation of SWOT, and the origin remains unclear. The degree to which the internal environment of the firm matches with the external environment is expressed by the concept of strategic fit.

- Strengths: characteristics that give an advantage over others.
- Weaknesses: characteristics that place a disadvantage relative to others.
- Opportunities: elements that could exploit to its advantage.
- Threats: elements that could cause trouble in the long run

Identification of SWOTs is important to businesses because they can inform later steps in planning to achieve an objective. As it pertains to relationships, it lets us know what we bring to the table and what areas we need to work on as an individual.

Chapter 6 is less about reading and more about assessing and writing about who you are. Your Strengths, your weakness, your opportunities, your threats. Being realistic about who you really are and not only what you wanted people to know about you.

- What are your strengths that you bring to a relationship?
- What are you weaknesses that may damage a relationship?
- What are your opportunities that expand the possibilities and future goals in a relationship?
- What are threats from your past and personality that could damage a relationship?

Years after, I learned of SWOT in the business world and I decided to apply it to my personal life. I learned more about myself after going through a divorce and having to re-enter the dating scene. I wanted to be real about who I was and be honest with the person that I wanted to date. Lying and misrepresenting myself would only get me in trouble in the long run and would trigger issues in a relationship and may cause the relationship to end somewhere down the line. To be honest that actually happened.

Here are a few questions that will help you understand and know your own SWOT assessment:

63

Strengths

- What do you do best?
- What do other people compliment about you the most?
- Which of your achievements are you most proud of?
- What values do you believe?
- How influential are you within your circle of friends and family?

Weaknesses

- What issues do you usually avoid in a relationship because you don't feel confident about handling them?
- What will the people around you see as your weaknesses?
- What are you insecurities?
- What are your negative habits (for example, are you often late, are you disorganized, do you have a short temper, or are you poor at handling stress)?
- Do you have personality traits that hold you back?

Again, consider this from a personal/internal perspective and an external perspective. Do other people see weaknesses that you don't see? Do friends, family members or previous partners bring up certain issues repeatedly? Be realistic – it's best to face any unpleasant truths as soon as possible.

Opportunities

- What future goals do you have?
- Do you have a plan for your future?
- Have you honestly addressed any of your weaknesses?
- What life lessons have you learned from your mistakes?
- Do you have an accountability partner?

Threats

- What weaknesses have you not addressed?
- Do you have unresolved issues with friends or family?
- Are you unwilling to change?
- Do you always think you're right?

A SWOT assessment is an outline for analyzing your strengths and weaknesses as well as the opportunities and threats that you may face. This will help you focus on your strengths, minimize your weaknesses, take the greatest possible advantage of opportunities, and address your threats in a relationship. Take the time to answer these questions. Write your answers and review them. Look deep within and rediscover who you are.

Chapter 7

Beyond the Body?

Your most attractive feature isn't physical, it's internal.

As a child, I remember hearing stories and fairy tales that ended with phrases like… "And they lived happily ever after". The phrase was cemented in my head from these stories. It also shaped my thinking; causing me to later ponder as an adult and ask the question, what does happily ever after look like? I soon found out as a young adult that there is no such thing as happily ever after. Another thing that had cemented in my head was some of the moral lessons that came with those fairy tales. Several stories had an undertone meaning or moral message. I remember teachers closing the book and saying this phrase…."And the moral of the story is…?" And that's when kids from my class would scream out what they had learned from the story. Thinking back, it was funny how those lessons stayed with me. One lesson or story that stayed with me was the story of "Beauty and the Beast." Now there have been several versions and adaptations to the story but the story remains that same. The story goes a little something like this. A merchant exchanges his youngest daughter for his freedom. The merchant has 3 daughters. One night, he becomes lost in the woods. Looking for shelter, he enters a great big lavish palace. A hidden figure opens the giant doors and silently invites him in. The merchant finds tables inside laden with food and drink, which had been left for him by the palace's hidden owner. The merchant accepts this gift and spends the night in the palace. The next morning, as the merchant is about to leave, he sees a rose garden and recalls that Belle, his youngest daughter loved roses. When he picked up the loveliest rose he can find, the merchant is confronted by a hideous "Beast" which tells him that for taking his most precious possession after accepting his hospitality, the merchant must die. (That sucks) The merchant begs to be set free, arguing that he had only picked the rose as a gift for his youngest daughter. The Beast agrees to let him give the rose to Belle, but only if Belle would return in his place.

The merchant is upset, but accepts this condition. The Beast sends him on his way, with jewels and fine clothes for his daughters, and stresses that Belle must never know about his deal. The merchant, upon arriving home, tries to hide the secret from Belle, but she pries it from him and willingly goes to the Beast's castle. The Beast receives her graciously and informs her that she is now mistress of the palace, and he is her servant. He gives her lavish clothing and food and carries on lengthy conversations with her. Every night, the Beast asks Belle to marry him, only to be refused each time. After each refusal, Belle dreams of a handsome prince who pleads with her to answer why she keeps refusing him, to which she replies that she cannot marry the Beast because she loves him only as a friend. Belle does not make the connection between the handsome prince and the Beast and becomes convinced that the Beast is holding the prince captive somewhere in the castle. She searches and discovers multiple enchanted rooms, but never the prince from her dreams. Now all the while she was thinking that the man of her dreams was a handsome prince.

For several months, Belle lives a life of luxury at the Beast's palace, having every whim catered to by servants, with no end of riches to amuse her and an endless supply of exquisite finery to wear. Eventually, she becomes homesick and begs the Beast to allow her to go see her family. He allows it on the condition that she returns exactly a week later. Belle

agrees to this and sets off for home with an enchanted
mirror and ring. The mirror allows her to see what is going
on back at the Beast's castle, and the ring allows her to
return to the castle in an instant when turned three times
around her finger. Her older sisters are surprised to find her
well fed and dressed in finery. They are envious when they
hear of her happy life at the castle, and, hearing that she
must return to the Beast on a certain day, beg her to stay
another day, even putting onion in their eyes to make it
appear as though they are weeping. They hope that the Beast
will be angry with Belle for breaking her promise and eat her
alive. Belle's heart is moved by her sisters' false show of love,
and she agrees to stay. Belle begins to feel guilty about
breaking her promise to the Beast and uses the mirror to see
him back at the castle. She is horrified to discover that the
Beast is lying half-dead from heartbreak near the rose
bushes her father had stolen from and she immediately uses
the ring to return to the Beast.

Belle weeps over the Beast, saying that she loves him. When
her tears strike him, the Beast is transformed into the
handsome prince from Belle's dreams. The Prince informs
her that long ago, a fairy turned him into a hideous beast
after he refused to let her in from the rain, and that only by
finding true love, despite his ugliness, could the curse be

broken. He and Belle are married and they live happily ever after together. (LOL)

Over the course of the months that Belle spent with the Beast, she got an opportunity to get to know him, however her heart was blinded by what her eyes saw. She was looking with her eyes and not her heart. Her eyes saw a beastly man that catered to her every extravagant desire. She was open to take advantage of his things and possessions but not open to see his heart of generosity, and how he was a loving and caring man. The true prince that she was looking for stood right in front of her face, all she had to do was close her eyes. Many of us hold on to the thought of finding that special someone and living happily ever after but some of us have forgotten about the lessons that some of our favorite fairy tales have tried to teach us as well.

I have another fairy tale that has given me some life lessons as well, however, I wasn't a child when I learned of this story. I was actually a married and the father of my own children. The story became of pop culture classic. It was an animated story made by DreamWorks Pictures. The story was Shrek. This movie was funny and entertaining from start to finish. But in writing this book, I thought about the lessons of my fairy tale years again. Shrek, a green ogre who loves the solitude in his swamp, finds his life interrupted when many fairytale characters are exiled there by order of the fairytale-hating Lord Farquaad. Shrek tells them that he will go ask Farquaad to send them back. He brings along a talking Donkey who is the only fairytale creature who knows the way to Duloc.

Meanwhile, Farquaad tortures the Gingerbread Man into giving the location of the remaining fairytale creatures until his guards rush in with something he has been searching for: the Magic Mirror. He asks The Mirror if his kingdom is the fairest of them all but he's told that he's not even a king. To be a king, he must marry a princess and is given three options, from which he chooses Princess Fiona, who is locked in a castle tower guarded by lava and a dragon. The Mirror tries to mention "the little thing that happens at night" but was unsuccessful. Shrek and Donkey arrive at Farquaad's palace in Duloc, where they end up in a tournament. The winner gets the "privilege" of rescuing Fiona so that Farquaad may marry her. Shrek and Donkey easily defeat the other knights in wrestling-match fashion, and Farquaad accepts his offer to move the fairytale creatures from his swamp if Shrek rescues Fiona.

Shrek and Donkey travel to the castle and split up to find

Fiona. Donkey encounters the dragon and sweet-talks the beast before learning that it is female. Dragon takes a liking to him and carries him to her chambers. Shrek finds Fiona, who is appalled at his lack of romanticism. As they leave, Shrek saves Donkey, caught in Dragon's tender clutches, and forces her to chase them out of the castle. At first, Fiona is thrilled to be rescued but is quickly disappointed when Shrek reveals he is an ogre.

As the three journey to Duloc, Fiona urges the two to camp out for the night while she sleeps in a cave. Shrek and Donkey stargaze while Shrek tells stories about great ogres and says that he will build a wall around his swamp when he returns. When Donkey persistently asks why, he says that everyone judges him before knowing him; therefore, he feels he is better off alone, despite Donkey's admission that he did immediately judge him when they met.

Along the way, Shrek and Fiona find they have more in common and start liking each other. From out of nowhere feelings had begun to develop. The trio is almost at Duloc, and that night Fiona shelters in a windmill. When Donkey hears a strange noise coming from the windmill, he finds Fiona turned into an ogre. She explains her childhood curse and transforms each night, which is why she was locked away, and that only her true love's kiss will return her to her "love's true form." Shrek, about to confess his feelings for

Fiona with a sunflower, partly overhears them, and is heartbroken as he mistakes her disgust with her transformation to an "ugly beast" as disgust with him. Fiona makes Donkey promise not to tell Shrek, vowing to do it herself. The next morning, Shrek has brought Lord Farquaad to Fiona. The couple return to Duloc, while a hurt Shrek angrily leaves his friendship with Donkey and returns to his now-vacated swamp, remembering what Fiona "said" about him.

Despite his privacy, Shrek is devastated and misses Fiona. Furious at Shrek, Donkey comes to the swamp where Shrek says he overheard Donkey and Fiona's conversation. Donkey keeps his promise to Fiona and tells Shrek that she was talking about someone else. He accepts Shrek's apology and tells him that Fiona will be getting married soon, urging Shrek into action to gain Fiona's love. They travel to Duloc quickly, thanks to Dragon, who had escaped her confines and followed Donkey.

Shrek interrupts the wedding before Farquaad can kiss Fiona. He tells her that Farquaad is not her true love and only marrying her to become king. The sun sets, which turns Fiona into an ogre in front of everyone in the church, causing Shrek to fully understand what he overheard. Outraged by Fiona, Farquaad orders Shrek killed and Fiona detained. Shrek whistles for Dragon who bursts in along with Donkey and devours Farquaad. Shrek and Fiona profess their love and share a kiss; Fiona is bathed in light as her curse is broken but is surprised that she is still an ogre, as she thought she would become beautiful, to which Shrek replies that she is beautiful. They marry in the swamp and leave on their honeymoon. The moral to this story is that real beauty is in the eye of the beholder. Shrek was able to see her beauty even if she was an ogre or a princess. The essence of who she really was, was not on her exterior, it lied within her. She was the one with the hang-ups of her appearance. Our society has given us the illusion that physical appearance is everything. We have become so concerned with our physical appearance until some women have actually died from plastic surgery, Botox, butt injections, etc. The real you is underneath the clothing and underneath the shell we call a body. Princess Fiona was able to live in her true beauty when someone was able to see it beyond her body.

Quite a number of times, we seem to forget the moral message but cling to the last line of most fairy tales, "And they lived happily ever after". There is no such thing as happily ever after in the real world. The real world lasts longer than a few pages of a book or longer than a few hours at the movies. When we close the book and leave the theater, the true question is, "what have I learned and how can I apply this to my life?" I know some of you may be saying that these are just fairy tales and they hold no real value. I will have to disagree with you. Don't be blind like Belle and don't devalue the true essence of the story like Princess Fiona. Open your heart to what the stories are saying and trying to teach us. When looking for and waiting for a mate, we must look beyond the body. We have covered part of this in the book already in the values vs. desire section; however, I felt it's necessary to address it again. Your prince or princess may be right within your reach but you refuse to look with your heart rather than just looking with your eyes......Look beyond the body.

Section 2:

**Highway of Dating
Every road is a journey, the question is
where are you going?**

Chapter 8

They Judge me, they judge me not

Judging people does not define what type of person they are, it defines what type of person you are.

Divorce court, Judge Judy, Judge Joe Brown, The People's Court, Judge Mathis, Judge Mills Lane, and Judge Alex etc..... I could go one but I won't. It seems our society is in love with court TV and judgment. I remember as a child watching People's court with my mother, the music would come on and the plaintiff would walk in. You would hear their story and why they were there; then the defendant would come in and you would hear their side of the story. There were always two sides of the story and the judge had to decipher whose story was more believable. As humans, we can be very judgmental; but in a relationship being judgmental can create an uneasy environment. But why are we so judgmental? Judging in a relationship is based on opinion of circumstances that are presented in the mind. Your

We have a tendency to marry our feelings but only date the facts in our relationships.

judgment will be the result of your thoughts, experiences and feelings. You have to determine what are fact, fiction and the truth. A courtroom judgment is mainly based on facts and passing judgment on the guidelines of the law. In a relationship, judgment is mainly based on feelings and feelings have no guidelines. Now don't get me wrong, facts will have an influence but feelings typically have more pull in a relationship. We have a tendency to marry our feelings but only date the facts in our relationships. Facts can lead us to the truth, but feelings can be misleading.

When dating someone, his or her past comes with them to the relationship. It would be ideal to get that person fresh out of the box with no marks, no dings, not refurbished; no past relationships, no childhood issues, etc. but people come in to a relationship with a history. Maybe it's a history of abuse and low self-esteem; what about a history of entitlement or a history of lack and neglect. Even a history of good things is still history and will show up in a relationship. The list could be infinite. But their past has shaped and molded them to who they are today. If you're dating someone, you're typically interested in them for a reason or you wouldn't be dating them. It was something about them that drew you. Every person has a past but not every person lives in their past. Is it fair to pass judgment on your partner if their past has some issues? A person's past can tell you where they have been but it doesn't always indicate where they are going.

Have you ever been in a relationship and the person was so judgmental? They are critical of everything you do or say. They pass judgment before hearing all the facts. They sometimes create a hostile environment. How did it make you feel? If you have never been in that type of situation where you felt judged, maybe you are the one doing the judging. I have personally been on both sides of the gavel in a relationship. I have been judged and I have been the judge. In retrospect, both are neither are a good place to be in a relationship. I have learned that creating a non-judgment zone in a relationship has major benefits and allows you to experience a great level of freedom and connection within your relationship. What's a non-judgment zone in a relationship? It's a realm of communication and interaction with each other that you and your partner create. In this realm, you don't judge each other's past; you can

A person's past can tell you where they have been but it doesn't always indicate where they are going.

come to each other with your most deep and darkest secrets and not worry about judgment from your partner. Now before we get into creating this non-judgment zone and what it takes; we must first understand where judgment in a relationship comes from, why we do it and how we must handle it. Judgment in a relationship can come from a variety of places. I want to focus on 5 major places where judgment can arise.

Judgment comes from:

- Differences – We are different for a reason
- Hurt – When we hurt we pass judgment
- Protection – Not wanting to be hurt again
- Projection – Projecting our views and feelings on our partner
- Control – Our judgment may influence their actions.

Differences

When you take two people raised differently and from different backgrounds, you are going to have a difference of opinion. Those differences open up the door for judgment. When I was married, I remember the first argument my ex-wife and I had. It was a Saturday morning and I got up early to get some chores done. I went to wake my new bride up to do chores on a Saturday and she was angry with me. She was upset because it was a Saturday and she wanted to sleep in. Saturday to me meant chores. Our differences caused friction and an argument. In addition to an argument, judgment was also passed by both of us. I judged her as being lazy and she judged me as being inconsiderate and selfish. Because of my immaturity at the time, I didn't have a proper solution to compromise to make it a win-win situation for both of us, thus resentment setting in between us. This situation could have had an easy fix but it grew into more judging and friction in the relationship. When there are differences in a relationship, the goal should be to find balance. We are different for a reason. Differences can bring balance when those differences are understood. We don't all have to be the same but we do need to find the balance in our relationships. It's not the differences that divide us, it's our inability to celebrate and embrace those differences. Don't judge your partner for being different, find a way to compliment that difference. Create a win-win option for both of you. If there is no way for a win-win to happen, someone will have to be the bigger person and concede for the betterment of the relationship. You can either be right or be the relationship; which is more important?

Hurt

One definition of hurt is "the damage or decrease in efficiency". Many people have been damaged by childhood experiences, life experiences and previous relationships, which hurt and left them scarred. When we are hurt and allow that hurt to stay in our lives, every relationship will suffer from that pain. The hurt will serve as a filter on how we interact, communicate and assess any information. It's important that we deal with pain from other relationships and past experiences before we try to enter a new relationship. Confronting the pain will allow us not to judge the present relationship from a previous

your current partner should not pay for the mistakes of a previous partner

partner. After my divorce, I was now a single man with the ability to date. Dating after being married for 16 years was a new experience. I re-entered the dating world but I was not ready for what I would experience in meeting new people. I quickly found out that women were carrying around hurt from previous relationships that would hinder them from being in a new healthy relationship or give a new relationship a valid chance. Music Soul Child sung a song entitled "Previous Cats". One of the lines in the song says: "I'm not to blame for the pain

Who had your heart before me, girl no
That was caused by previous cats
You got to see me for me"

Simply put, your current partner should not pay for the
mistakes of a previous partner.

You have to begin to let that go. Letting go may not be easy
always but it is always worth it. Now I am not being
judgmental on women. Men hold onto the past relationships
and things as well. This goes for both male and female. LET
IT GO!! Some of you may be asking, how do I let it go? The
first thing to remember is that. you cannot conquer what you
are afraid to confront.

The next order of business is to acknowledge the pain. You
Understand that the pain has affected you. You may have
adopted certain behaviors and not even realized what you
are doing because the reaction to the pain has become a part
of you. After you acknowledge the pain, you must forgive the
person that caused the pain. Forgiveness does not change
the past, but it will free you for your future. If you are free,
you will be free not to judge your partner based on a previous
relationship or childhood experience.

you cannot conquer what you are afraid to confront.

83

Protection

Judging from protection is a direct result of being hurt. We judge because we are trying to protect ourselves from being hurt again. While writing this book, I had a conversation with a female friend. I had not seen her in a while so she caught me up about her new man of interest. She began to tell me what she liked about him and everything he came to the table with. She liked him but she was reluctant to tell him how she really felt. She didn't want to make herself too available and too vulnerable. She had been hurt before in the past from a previous relationship and didn't like the fact of being vulnerable again. It had been some time since she dated and was not sure if she wanted to place her heart into the hand of a man. It seemed that every time she would become vulnerable with a man she would get hurt in turn. She would sabotage her own relationships. She would judge the man on a potential problem and make it his fault why the relationship wouldn't work. The protection of herself was the worst enemy to making progress within any relationship. As I listened to her reflect over the relationships in her past, she realized that she misjudged a few men from her past because she was trying to protect her heart. Judging others to protect you is not only selfish but it is dangerous in the long run. The only one really getting hurt is you. After I pointed out to her what she was doing, she realized that it would take some time for her to stop judging her new friend but understood that in order to move forward she would have to take down some of the walls that she had built to protect herself.

Projection

Projection is a common behavior we see in couples that have been together for a while. Whatever energy a person is feeling, they transfer that energy to the other person. In a relationship, we have a tendency to disown qualities we don't like about ourselves and see those qualities in our partner. Projection can be a very disrupting and damaging behavior in a relationship. One example of this could be if your partner accuses you of being selfish because you take time for yourself away from the cares of life and other responsibilities. However, your partner wishes they could take a break from all the cares of their life. They want to escape their responsibilities but they believe that this action would be selfish. So they resent you and judge you for being selfish because they haven't taken any time for themselves like they wish they could. No matter how you respond, it will be wrong, thus setting off a chain reaction of more judgment and confusion. If we project our negative energy on our partner and try to make them feel less adequate because of our issues, that is classic projection. The way to overcome this problem is to look within and not without. If we have an issue with something that our partner does, make sure it's not self-issue that we are just projecting onto them. Michael Jackson had a song called "Man in the Mirror". One line from the song was:

"If You Wanna Make The
World A Better Place
Take A Look At Yourself And
Then Make That . . .
Change!"

Be the change you want to see in your partner.

Control

If control were a mathematical equation, it would be;

Fear +Unknown + Insecurity = Desire for Control.

One of the best ways to try to control someone in a relationship is to try to pass judgment on them to manipulate their actions. When we don't know something, we can get scared. When fear comes into play coupled with a person's insecurity we want to dictate what should happen.

Relationships can be filled with challenges of the unknowns. What if you partner loses their job? What about instead of losing a job they get a promotion that would cause them to move out of state? When unknown life episodes happen, fear is a common response. Your fear is a reflection that you want to be in control and it also reveals something that you are insecure about. Partners use control to try to persuade situations and circumstances in their favor. Elizabeth and Brian had been dating for 10 months. When they first met, Elizabeth did not have a car. This was not an issue for Brian. After 2 months of dating, Brian began to take and pick up Elizabeth from work. Her job was on the way to his job so it was pretty easy for him to make it work. Brian enjoyed the rides as it gave them a chance to talk about their day and connect to and from work. After 6 months of this, Elizabeth finally got her own car and was excited about not having to burden Brian with picking her up and dropping her to work. At first, Brian was happy for Elizabeth but that soon changed. Now that Elizabeth had her own car, it seemed that there quality time had diminished. Elizabeth would now run errands and go out with her friends instead of just hanging out with Brian. With Brian driving Elizabeth to and from work, he subconsciously had a desire to control. With Elizabeth having a car now, it also exposed a level of insecurity and fear within Brian. His desire to control her actions caused Brian to pass judgment on Elizabeth. He was concerned that she may have been doing something she was not supposed to, during their time away from each other. This was not the case at all. In a previous relationship, Brian had been cheated on. Brian feared losing his relationship and didn't know any other way but to be controlling and judgmental towards Elizabeth. Brian had to learn that controlling and judgment were not the way to handle his issues of fear and insecurity. One thing that allowed Brian to overcome this was letting go of the hurt from the previous relationship and being honest with Elizabeth about how he felt. When he confronted his fear and insecurity, he was able to conquer it.

Creating a "No Judgment Zone" within a relationship is not an easy task. We have listed the things that cause judgment but now I want to discuss what it takes to make it actually happen. In addition, you will also find tools to overcome some of the causes we listed.

No Judgment zone
- Maturity
- Compartmentalize
- Inventory of motives

- Friendship
- Don't expect what you can't provide

Maturity

It is a dangerous thing for a immature person to be in a relationship. Maturity is more about mindset than it is age. One definition for maturity is "full growth or development". Immaturity is something that I see commonly is several couples from young to older couples. Rather than looking at the big picture of the relationship, they choose to focus on the minor aspects of a situation which leads to weighing down the entire relationship. Let me be clear, it's the little things that will make or break a relationship. However, we can put too much energy into things that can be small in comparison to the overall relationship. So what distinguishes a mature person from an immature person in a relationship? As it pertains to this aspect of the relationship, I want to use an infant child to paint a picture. There are two characteristics of an infant child that are signs of immaturity:

- Inability to communicate or express themselves properly
- Pouting or crying when their way does not happen

If you respond to issues like this, you are showing signs of immaturity. If your partner handles himself or herself like this then they are displaying signs of immaturity. A mature person knows how to communicate and get his point across and does not resort to uncontrollable emotional behavior to get his way. Being mature gives a person the ability to stay on task and focus on the main objective of the relationship.

As it pertains to judgment in a relationship; an immature person wants to judge his partner, a mature person wants to help his partner grow and develop.

Chris had a secret when he met Kathy. They had been dating for seven months and things were going well. With things going well, Chris was at a tug-of-war with his feelings and his secret that he wanted to share but didn't know how. He didn't want to do anything that would jeopardize his

> As it pertains to judgment in a relationship; an immature person wants to judge his partner, a mature person wants to help his partner grow and develop.

relationship with Kathy. Seven months into the relationship, Chris wanted to go deeper and share his secret with Kathy, but he felt if he did, she wouldn't handle it correctly or she would judge him. Chris had shared his secret before with girls he dated but they started treating him differently afterwards. Revealing his secret usually led to the end of his relationships. Chris didn't want to be treated differently or judged; he just wanted to be understood. Chris was at a point of building his maturity yet testing Kathy's. How would she respond? What will she think of me? These were some of the questions that went through Chris' mind. Chris finally made the decision to share his secret. He loved Kathy and didn't want anything to come in between them thus damaging their future. After weeks of going over and over in his head what he would say; Chris finally shared his secret. Chris sat Kathy down one day in a park and told her that he had served five years in prison for possession of drugs with the intent to distribute. Chris was a former drug dealer and had been to prison. This was a shock to Kathy and she was silent for minute. She was at a pivotal moment where she could easily judge Chris or she could listen to all the facts of his past and accept him for the man he is today. When Kathy broke her silence, her first words were, "Thank you for telling me."

What would have been your first response? Would you have been able to keep calm from hearing a dark secret about your partner's past?

After her silence, she began to ask series of questions about his past and how this came about. Chris was very candid and shared some of his intimate secrets. He was tempted to lie but knew that would only create more challenges so he was honest about the details of his past. He also explained why it took him some time to share this information. Chris made a choice to be mature and properly express himself. Kathy made the choose to be mature and not judge Chris from his past but seek to understand him and the choices he had made at that time in his life. When both partners in a relationship make the choice to be mature, they open the door to possibilities of connecting with their partner. However, if you are dealing with a partner that is immature or you are honest with yourself and are immature, then trouble is on the horizon. Being mature in a relationship is a process and may take time. Infants don't come out the womb walking, they learn to roll over, and then sit up, and later crawl, then stand, and finally walk. It is all a process, and patience in the process is needed. Being mature prior to going into a relationship is great, but your maturity will be tested once you are in a relationship. Just as a baby may stumble or even fall when learning to walk, there will be moments where immaturity will feel like the right response but don't give in into your feelings.

After the meeting, Chris and Kathy both showed promise of maturity and I believe they have the tools and mindset to carry out their maturity within their relationship. Kathy made the choice to not judge Chris but to help him continue to develop. She could have judged him based on his past but she saw that his heart was sincere and appreciated his forwardness and honesty. Chris forwardness and honest laid the foundation for him to communicate with his partner. His maturity was met with maturity.

Selah Moment:

- Do you consider yourself mature or immature?
- What are some areas of your life that you could improve upon your maturity level?
- What are some things that would help you mature?

Compartmentalize

When dealing with issues of judgment in a relationship, sometimes a partner will lump all the issues of the relationship into his/her bag of judgment. Every occurrence or every issue from previous situations shows up in a discussion and causes more judgment. It's like having a bag of socks; you may be looking for one pair but you dump out the entire bag out and sift through all the socks to find just one pair. If the socks were in order, you could select the right pair of socks without dumping out the entire bag. When we lump our issues of a relationship all in one bag, we never solve any one issue, we simply continue fighting all the issues and never making progress. The weight of all issues of a relationship can cause people to judge their partner. Have you ever dated someone that every time an issue happened, they would bring up old issues or other challenges from the relationship that didn't have anything to do with the present issue? This form of judging can cause serious issues in a relationship but is also frustrating. A relationship stuck in the past cannot move forward.

Being able to compartmentalize issues of the relationship helps a relationship maintain its strength and empowers a couple to move forward. Ok, I hear some of you saying, "Well, what if it is the same issue over and over again?" If a partner is having the same issues over and over again, the key is to find out what triggers those issues. Determining what triggers a behavior is the first step to understanding and overcoming many issues. If your partner is not willing to discover their triggers then they may not be ready for a serious relationship. Understanding yourself through personal self-analysis is key to being a mature individual. It takes mature people in order to have mature relationships. Mature relationships don't allow themselves to get stuck

A relationship stuck in the past cannot move forward.

in issues. They focus on moving forward, developing and growing within the relationship and as individuals.

Being able to compartmentalize in a relationship is a helpful way to stay away from judging a partner. Here are four strategies to help you overcome the temptation of lumping all your issues together.

- Isolate – Separate all previous issues or any unresolved issues from the present issue. Focus your energy on the present issue. Don't bring up any other previous issues until the issue at hand has totally been resolved.

- Investigate – Make sure you have all the facts and the correct information pertaining to an issue. Don't make any assumptions about anything. Always ask open-ended questions to create a dialogue. Stay away from yes or no questions. Mature people ask questions, immature people make assumptions

- Interpret – Remember I talked about triggers? Understanding why a person does what they do is more important than what is being done. Finding the triggers helps us get to the root of a problem. Understanding your partner's triggers is key to interpreting the real problems.

- Implement – Anyone can tell you that you have a flat tire. The difference is if you can help me change the tire. If you come to your partner with an issue, always being ready and willing to bring a solution. Don't just expose the problem, be a helper to solve it.

There is no easy road to dealing with issues in a relationship but having a GPS in the car makes the journey a little better.

Inventory of motives

When you understand your 'why,' your 'what' becomes easier. I once heard a story of a comedian. He was at a large venue and began to tell people about his purpose. He had recently understood his purpose and wanted to share it with is audience. He begin to ask members in the audience their profession and what industry they worked in. One gentleman he talked to was a music director. Upon finding out his profession, he wanted to know if the music director knew how to sing. He asked the gentleman to sing a hymn. The music director complied and sang the classic hymn 'Amazing Grace.' With a deep robust voice, the man began to sing and he sound good.   When he finished singing, the comedian then gave him another set of instructions. The comedian told him to now sing like his uncle had just been released from prison or that he had escaped a near death experience of being shot in the head. Without hesitation, the music director belted out an even more robust, soulful, and meaningful rendition of the classic 'Amazing Grace.' The first time he asked him to sing, he knew what to sing but the second time he knew why he was singing.

If you have ever judged your partner, knowing you judged them is not as important as why you judged them. What were your motives to being judgmental? Was your judgment coming from a place of hurt, control or projecting etc.? The 'what' is not the issue, the 'why' is. In creating a non-judgment zone in a relationship, it's important to stay away from the causes of judgment;

- Differences
- Hurt
- Protection

- Projection
- Control

If these are you reasons to judge then you're not looking for a relationship you're looking for a fight.

Friendship

A true friend accepts you for who you are, but also helps you become who you should be. This statement could not be truer than in the confines of a dating relationship. Over the course of a relationship, you have the potential to become the best friends. One thing I love about the friends I have in my life is that they have the ability to tell me when I'm wrong. More important than telling me when I'm wrong, is how they tell me. They tell me in love. If you are in a relationship, friendship must be a vital component of your relationship. If you can't be true friends, how can you be true lovers? Real friends don't judge each other, they help each other. One of the best routes to make a relationship work is to be friends first. I took a pre-marital class while writing this book and they spoke on friendship very highly. Friendship should be the first step in the courting process. While in the class, the instructor gave these things that a friendship should be:

- Friends TRUST each other

- Friends FORGIVE each other
- Friends are HONEST with each other
- Friends COMMUNICATE frequently
- Friends HAVE LOVE for each other
- Friends keep each other ACCOUNTABLE
- Friends PROTECT each other
- Friends don't CONTROL each other

And I will add this last one…. Friends don't JUDGE each other. As a relationship grows, you desire to help each other be accountable not judge each other. You want the best for your partner but not by putting them down in judgment. If your heart is sincere, you should always speak to your partner in love not in judgment. They are your friend not your enemy.

Don't expect what you can't provide

If you don't want to be judged, you should not judge anyone. After my marriage ended, I was thrust into dating, however, people and dating had changed since I got married. I could remember a young lady I dated, who would constantly tell me what was wrong with me. Seemed like I didn't do anything right. She would jump to conclusions and make assumptions about me frequently. I constantly felt judged

99

and was uncomfortable with talking to her about things in an effort not to be judged. I would keep things private and thus limiting our ability to communicate. Toward the end of our dating and courting, I asked her a question about the way she talked to me. She turned it around and told me I was judging her because she was not raised in a Christian home like me and I was condemning her. Now I was not condemning her in any way but when I confronted her about an issue I was having, she felt judge. She was feeling what I was feeling from her all this time and she didn't like it at all. This discussion turned into an argument and needless to say we are not together anymore. She could not eat a dish that she was constantly serving. She didn't want to feel like she was being judged but was constantly in the judgment chair ready to slam her gavel and judge me. You must be careful what you give out, because it will return to you eventually. If you don't want to be judged, you should be careful not to judge anyone.

Learn to take responsibility for your flaws and stop judging everyone for theirs. Judge not, that you will not be judged... Selah

This chapter was one of the hardest chapters for me to write in this book. I have a pet peeve of being judged. I experienced judgment and misunderstanding in my marriage. I experienced judgment and misunderstanding when I started dating again. It caused me not to want to share any of my feelings and secrets in an effort of not being judged. However, it was through that judgment and experiences that I discovered the things about me that needed to be adjusted. I discovered some of my shortcomings, flaws and mistakes that I have made along the way. In my discovery I made the decision to be better and not bitter. If you are not learning from your mistakes then, maybe that's why you keep repeating them. If you didn't learn anything form your last relationship then, maybe that's why you keep having the same type of relationships.

Learn to take responsibility for your flaws and stop judging everyone for theirs. Judge not, that you will not be judged... Selah

Chapter 9

Freedom over Fear

Freedom is the ability for you to be you without anyone's permission or approval.

Diane was in the dressing room on a glorious spring afternoon preparing to marry the man of her dreams. He was tall, handsome and made a good living. This was the day she had dreamed about since she was a small child. She wanted everything perfect. Diane had to have the right flowers so the pushed their wedding back a few weeks so that the flowers would be at their optimal bloom. She ordered her dress and went to get refitted 4 times just to make sure it was the perfect style and fit. She had been exercising and dieting for 6 months to make sure her body was in tip top shape for this momentous occasion. Her family and soon to be husband spared no expense to make sure everything was perfect. As she sat in the waiting room, she asked a bridal party to give her some time alone. She wanted to just pray by herself as she prepared to be Mrs. Lyons. Seated in the blush-cushioned chair, she looked at herself in the mirror and thought to herself that today was the best day of her life. Her makeup was flawless, her gown was perfect, and her hair didn't have a strand out of place. As she closed her eyes to pray, she thought to herself, this is the beginning of a beautiful fairy tale wedding and life. With her hands folded and eyes closed she prayed... "Lord, thank you for this beautiful day. I pray that everything goes according to plan and that this day be just like I've imagined it would be. Amen" As she opened her eyes, she heard a little small voice in her head. The voice sad "Don't marry this man." Shocked and bothered she said to herself, "oh that's just wedding day jitters." She heard it again this time a little louder. "Don't marry this man." From her religious upbringing, she stopped and said "God is that you?" She heard it a 3rd time and the voice said the same thing, only this time the voice said her name and a little bit more. "Diane, don't marry this man, he is not the one I have for you." Scared and afraid she called for Tracy, her maid of honor and her maid of honor looked at her like she was crazy and told her to just calm down, it's just wedding day jitters. Tracy got her some water and told her to relax because everything was going to be ok. Diane was beginning to unravel; her perfect day was taking a turn for the worst. She asked to be alone again and Tracy left her alone. Diane began to rationalized everything and question everything. She considered; if she didn't marry today, she would have wasted money, her family would be humiliated, what would her fiancé think? People would think she was crazy. How do you call off a wedding that is about to start? Was God talking to her or was she just having wedding day jitters. She was scared to call off the wedding because if she didn't get married now, it would jeopardize her chances of having children because she was getting older. She thought of how long she waited for this relationship. Diane was afraid of being alone again. Sleeping alone, growing old alone. Question after question rolled over in her head. Diane looked at herself in the mirror and said, "I can't stop this wedding, its already in motion. I will just talk to my husband about what I heard and he will know what to do." So Diane walked down the aisle and married Richard her fiancé. The wedding was beautiful and perfect. The reception was everything she dreamed of. Her guest and family boosted how this wedding was so fabulous. Two years later, Richard and Diane were divorced. What happened? Richard was not the man he portrayed to be and ended up being abusive to Diane. Diane married Richard out of fear. She was allowing her emotions to dictate to her what she should do. Her fear of being alone.

Her fear of growing old alone, the fear of disappointing her family and guest. The emotions of fear were in the driver seat and drove her to a place she didn't want to be. The emotion of fear is only an indication of there is something wrong. When approaching a relationship, your actions should come from a place a freedom and not fear. There are times when people enter in relationships because of fear. There are times when people stay in relationships because of fear. Fear is not the right driver to have driving you around. The story of Diane and Richard is a true story, I changed the names in order to protect the identity, but the story is very real and it happens more often than you think. Many people don't believe in a higher power and that is understandable. Even Diane's close friend thought she was losing her mind for a second. If you tell people that God spoke to you, they would probably think you're crazy too. But how many times have you heard someone say "something told me not to do that" or "something told me not to go there" and in the end some type of adverse situation happens and the person feels bad because they didn't listen to the little small voice that they heard telling them to do or not to do something. The bigger picture in this case is fear was the motivating factor of Diane's actions.

Now, being honest with ourselves, let's answer this question. Have you ever stayed in a relationship because you were motivated by fear? That could be fear of being alone, fear of that person and what they may do. What about this? Have you ever treated someone that you were in a relationship with in a certain way as a protective mechanism for yourself because you were scared of that person hurting you? (Either physically or emotionally). You responded and acted out your fear because of what someone else did to you, and you said that no one would ever hurt you again. How about being mean to your partner because you thought they were trying to hurt you, so you wanted to hurt them first. All these things are being done from a place of fear. Fear is now in the driver seat and is in control of what you do in your relationship. Someone cheated on you, and now every person you get into a relationship with can't be trusted by you. A new relationship deserves a clean slate. The current person may not deserve you operating with them from a place of fear. They deserve your freedom. Freedom from past hurts and issues; Freedom from remorse and regret. Your emotional fear dictating your relationship will eat away at your relationship like a cancer.

I remember driving in the car with a group of friends. We were on our way to a party. I had the car, but the friends in the car knew where we were going. It was a house party of one of our friends whose house I had only been to once. I couldn't remember all the details to get to that house but I was familiar with the neighborhood. The passenger in the rear of the car was giving the directions. The passenger in the front of the car knew how to get there too, but there were some discrepancies on the route we were taking so we allowed the back seat driver to call the shots. The back seat driver was not the best in giving directions because they were busy talking and listening to music and often would tell me when to turn at the last minute. Because of the back seat driver's poor judgment, their license had been suspended so allowing them to drive was out of the question. I was left to depend on the person with poor judgment, lack of focus and questionable habits for directions. Needless to say we got lost and turned around a few times before I just asked for the address and plugged it into my GPS for turn-by-turn directions. In addition to that, when we got in the neighborhood, things started to look familiar and I was able to find the party using my GPS and memory.

As it pertains to a relationship, fear should always be in the back seat and never in the driver seat. I tell my children that the number 1 rule in life is not to be scared. The reason is that when you are scared, you don't make proper choices, your judgment is off and you have very little focus. Just like my back seat passenger. You may have experienced some hurt or pain from a previous situation or relationship, but you can't allow that hurt and fear of being hurt again dictate how your next relationship is going to be. Your current partner should not be paying the bill of your last partner's invoice.

So the question is how do we operate from a place a freedom?

Your fear in something is an indication that something from a previous relationship or circumstance has not healed. If you injure yourself and if someone touches your bruise and pain is present, that is an

Your current partner should not be paying the bill of your last partner's invoice.

indication that full healing has not taken place. If they touch the place where the bruise was and no pain comes, that indicates that full healing has happened. When you operate from a place of fear in a relationship, that indicates that there is an area in your life or emotions that needs to be healed. How do we begin to heal?

Let's Eat some Pie

Pie makes everybody feel good - Laurie Halse Anderson

My favorite Pie to eat is Sweet potato pie. It always makes me feel good and taste good. Well today we are going to eat a figurative Pie. P.I.E. is an acronym for Perception, Interpretation and Energy.

This P.I.E. will begin the healing process we need in order to get over some of the hurts we may have experienced from previous relationship challenges

Perception – Changing the way we look at what and who hurt us. Imagine running in the in woods. While running, you see what you perceive to be a snake. You immediately take off in a different direction because of the fear you have regarding snakes. Later you return and see that what you perceived to be a snake was only a rope. Your understanding of what you thought to be a snake was influenced by your fear. The rope had nothing to do with your fear but received the treatment as if it was dangerous. We must change our perception and perspective on how we look at things if we are going to start being free from what hurt is. A simple deeper look or slowing down to see what was really going on would have given you the proper perspective on the perceived fear. If we translate that to our personal relationship lives, we have to ask ourselves; Are you a victim or victor from what hurt you? The saying goes, "you win some you lose some," but the truth is, you win some you learn some. Everything you have experienced that tried to hurt you has only made you stronger. You have to make the choice of being better and not bitter. Changing your perception and perspective of what happened to you frees you to be healed from your hurt. You didn't lose in those situations, you learned something. So take what you learned and use it to be a better person. Hurt people hurt people. If you bring your hurt, pain and fear to your next relationship, you will end up hurting the person you are with and they didn't do anything to you. Don't make them pay for the hurt that someone else put you through.

Interpretation – While on a trip to Vegas, I ate at an Asian Thai restaurant. This place was a 5 star cuisine and had excellent reviews. I had been in Vegas for 3 days and experienced some of the best buffets in the world already so I wanted to experience something a little different. The atmosphere of the restaurant was very chic and modern. The lights were dim and it provided a very sexy atmosphere. When my server came, I was already sure of what I wanted to eat. I saw on the menu a selection that would give me the opportunity to taste a variety of foods and experience the menu from different perspectives. When my food came, it was an array of beautiful food. The arrangement of the meal was quite lovely and I was ready to make a mess of what the chef had prepared. While eating the food, I began to taste and savor every bite. I could literally taste all the herbs and spices that the chef had put in the food. My mouth began to have a party of flavors and spices. My tongue was

110

experiencing a variety of tastes I had never experienced before. My taste buds began to interpret what it was tasting. My interpretation of the herbs were that the chef wanted me to feel good about what I was eating. He thought of my taste buds as he mixed the ingredients. Now that might be far-fetched but think about it. We sometimes internalize what someone did to us thinking that they were trying to do something to us personally. We personalize everything and make it about us. That chef wasn't thinking about me; he was just following the recipe and making a great dish. I personalized the meal and made the meal all about me. Yes I ordered it and it was for me but the same dish someone could have ordered and may have not liked the meal. My point is this. Everything from a previous relationship was not always meant to hurt you intentionally. Some people didn't know how to relate to you and that's not your fault. It was a lesson learned. Begin to interpret things that you experience differently. Stop saying that things happened to you and say that you experienced some things. Your experiences develop character, your experiences makes you a professional. When you are a professional at certain things, it means you have mastered some things. Be a master of your mind rather than mastered by your mind. Don't allow your mind to create fearful responses in your life based on previous experiences. Interpret things as a learning experience. Personalizing and internalizing everything can create a range of emotions that could block your judgment.

Energy – Your energy belongs in the right space. If you have a pair of pants that had a hole in the pocket of those pants, would you knowingly place money or an important item in that pocket? I believe NO is the answer to that question. Then why do you put energy into an area of your lives that is not beneficial? When we operate in relationships from a place of fear and hold grudges against past issues and people; we are now placing money into a pocket that has a hole in it. The pocket is supposed to hold the money until the time we need it. If we reach into a pocket that has a hole in it, we will only have a negative outcome because what we needed is now gone. Placing energy into negativity and regret only gives you more fear and negativity not freedom. Your energy should be going into your freedom not your fear. The energy you are placing in your fear is only creating more fear. Real healing can take place when we place our energy into an area of our life where positive things can take place. Fear is an energy that contracts, Love is the energy that expands. Love comes from a place of freedom. You can't love and be fearful at the same time.

Section 2 – Highway of Dating

Every road is a journey the question is where are you going?

Chapter 10

What's it worth

Relationships are like balance sheets...... You have debits and credits. Debits are things that can take away from your relationship and credits are things that can add to your relationship. Think about making a deposit today.

When I was a small child, I remember hearing my uncle singing these words;

"But now you have left me,
Oh, how I cried, I keep crying
You don't miss your water
Till your well runs dry."

As a little boy, I never understood what my uncle was singing about. He would sing this song many times after a date with a young lady. Sometimes he would sing the song when he actually lost something and couldn't find it. When I got older and began to experience life a little more; the words of this song would ring in my ear. I started to understand what the song was really about. The lyrics of the song were made famous by an American R&B singer-songwriter legend Otis Redding. The lyrics referred to water as a metaphor of lost love. When the well was dry, the water was gone. When the woman was gone, the love was lost. He didn't appreciate the water that the well held means that he didn't appreciate the love that the women brought to his life. He didn't know what the relationship was worth until it was too late and the relationship was over. Ask yourself this question; what is your relationship worth? Billionaire and philanthropist Warren Buffet was quoted as saying "Price is what you pay, value is what you get". If this quote proves to be true; what price are you paying to add value to your relationship? What investments are you making to define the worth of your relationship? Our society has learned to seek time investing in houses, jobs, cars, clothes etc. You name it and we spend a large amount of time and resources investing in things and not people. We live for the dollar. In America it's printed on our currency, "In God we trust;" but how true is that statement? The declaration on the money we use in exchange for things is

You can spend all your life trying to accumulate things but never really have anything. You really didn't have things, but your things had you.

supposed to be a creed that we live by.

However, look at our actions and you will see that we tend to put our trust in things and not God. We have been consumed with spending and trying to get all we can but we can't take any of that stuff with us if we were to pass away. You can spend all your life trying to accumulate things but never really have anything. You really didn't have things, but your things had you. Your choices in life revolved around materialism and things that didn't add value to your life but took away from your life. You can't appreciate what you want, before you appreciate what you have. Learn to appreciate what you have before what you have depreciates.

As it pertains to relationships, whatever you put in is what you are going to get out. You can't expect to receive something from a relationship if you haven't put anything into it. If you have a bank account at Wells Fargo, and you have been making deposits in that account. You can't go to Bank of America and get the money that you have been depositing from another account. The same thing applies to a relationship, you can't expect a return in something that you haven't made any deposits or made an investment in. We understand currency as it pertains to money; but what is the currency of our relationships. What investments are you making in your relationship that you may reap a benefit in the long run?

You can't appreciate what you want, before you appreciate what you have. Learn to appreciate what you have before what you have depreciates.

In the book, "5 Love Languages" by Gary Chapman; Chapman suggest 5 expressions of a relationship that constitute as a love language. How one partner communicates love and how the other partner receives love. The Love Languages were listed as:

- Words of Affirmation – words of praise or compliments are what this person values the most. They value words more than action of their partner. People who love words of affirmation have a hard time forgiving their partner of negative words or insulting words.
- Acts of Service - People who see acts of service as the greatest expression of love, hearing the phrase "let me do that for you" is like hitting the jackpot! These individuals want their partners to notice that their

117

own responsibilities are grand and sometimes overwhelming and that a helping-hand every once-an-a-while shows love and care. Just as much as these individuals love acts of service, they do not deal well with broken promises and laziness, because it shows a lack of value for them.

- **Receiving Gifts** - Not all people who enjoy receiving gifts are "materialistic." This just means that for these personalities, love is equated with a tangible thing. The gift doesn't have to be extravagant or elaborate, but it does have to be meaningful and thoughtful.

- **Quality Time** - For some people, spending time with loved ones is their preferred love language. Whether it be a quiet lunch or an afternoon walk, spending quality time and being the focus of their undivided attention leaves them feeling satisfied and comforted more than words.

- **Physical Touch** - The language of physical touch doesn't only refer to physical touch and affection in the bedroom, but refers to the everyday physical connections, like handholding, kissing, and any type of re-affirming physical contact. A person who desires physical touch and affection isn't overly touchy-feely but for them, touch shows how much their partner cares for them.

118

Let's take a look at these expressions of love as currency. Not in the exchange sense but in the investment sense. These expressions of love are how many people define how they love their partner and how and if their partner loves them? If your partner is a person that likes to receive words of affirmation, than you should make investments of words of affirmation. If words of affirmation are not your thing, then words of affirmation now become not only an investment but also a sacrifice. It becomes a sacrifice because it's not about what you want or need but it's about what they want or need within your relationship. Making sacrifices takes practice and does not come easily to every person. What are you willing to give up? What are you willing to sacrifice for the sake of your relationship? What are you willing to invest to reap a benefit from the person you say you love? Is your relationship worth the time and resources it takes in order to make an investment? For men, this is typically more difficult. Men have a tendency to be more selfish. Men make investments, however, it's harder for a man to make a sacrifice. A man will spend his resources to get what he wants; however, it's harder for him to make a sacrifice if he doesn't get anything in return. Women on the other hand are designed to be nurturing thus making sacrifices a little bit easier for a woman. Women carry milk in their breast; they carry babies in their womb and carry eggs in the uterus for a cycle. Women are physically, emotionally and mentally designed to nurture. It's easier for a woman to make sacrifices because she is made that way by design. A woman is made to care about another human being because she is physically designed to nurture and care for another human life. Men are not designed that way so they have to be taught how to do that. Women, men need your patience. A man can be guided on how to invest and make sacrifices, however, he needs your patience in the process. Men, women need our thoughtfulness. They need you to think about what you are doing and how you do it. We have to be more thoughtful in the things we do and say to them. We are different for a reason and that is to bring balance to both of our lives. Remember in the realm of a relationship, our words and deeds can be viewed as currency. Not only in the capacity of exchange but also in the capacity of an investment into the relationship. Every investor that I know wants a good ROI.

In the early 2000's, I took an interest in real estate, investing and flipping houses for profits. Before actually completing any deal, I learned as much as I could from classes, webinars and mentors. One term that was consistent with all my classes and information I learned was ROI. (Return On

Investment) ROI is simply the benefit to the investor resulting from an investment of some resource. There has to be an investment in order for a return to occur. This applies to relationships as well, even in dating/courting. If you are in the courtship stage of a relationship, you and your partner are making an investment to the future of your relationship together. You are not together just to be

> *"Someone is sitting in the shade today because someone planted a tree a long time ago".*

together; you are together with the goal of a lifelong commitment to one another. Your ROI is each other. Learning, growing together and bringing balances to each other, for the benefit of your future together.

To quote Warren Buffet again; "Someone is sitting in the shade today because someone planted a tree a long time ago".

What you are doing right now in your dating life will either add or take away from your life in the future.

I quote Warren Buffett because he is famous for his great investment and returns. He understands what it means to make a great return on a quality investment. Making money through investments is not easy work but it's typically worth the time and resources it takes to get a great ROI. Some investments take time to mature and reap its full benefit.

Other investments may have a big return in a short period of time but the return rarely last long. That is the same in relationships. There is no need to rush; certain things will take time to mature. The longer it takes to mature the more value it will have.

Warren Buffett, the CEO and largest stockholder of Berkshire Hathaway, is consistently ranked among the world's wealthiest people. Buffett acquired Berkshire Hathaway through a series of wise investments and calculated moves to position himself as the majority owner in the company. These calculated moves took time and patience. His investments were for the future and not just for the present moment. Looking beyond his current condition for a massive ROI in the future. He knew the value of sacrificing the right now, for a greater benefit of later. If you invested $1,000 in Berkshire Hathaway in 1980, that amount would be $532,165 higher today. If you invested $1,000 in Berkshire Hathaway in 1990, that amount would be $29,785 higher today. These investments grew over time and their value grew with that time. You have to be willing to put in the work and time in for your relationship to reap value. Warren Buffett has a net worth of approximately $68 billion dollars. If you were to put a monetary value of your relationship, based on your investment and sacrifices you've made for your partner, what would be your net worth in your relationship?

We invest our resources in so many materialistic things but eventually the value of those things will depreciate. Our most valuable commodity are two things that we take for granted on a daily bases. People and time are our most valuable commodity. If you lose a house, you could replace it. If you lose a job, you could find another one. Even if you lose money, you could make it back over the course of time. However, time and people are two things that could not be replaced. When you lose time, you can't get it back. If you lose a loved one, no one can replace that person. So why do we take for granted the two commodities that can't be easily replaced. How about we start doing something different. Why don't we take the two most valuable commodities and combine them. Why don't we invest our time in the people that matter the most in our life. Let's start by investing in the partner we have chosen to be in a relationship with. What would your relationship be like if you made a quality investment into your partner? An investment that would have an ROI of a disgustingly beautiful relationship. Remember, every investment made now is a benefit for the future. The future you have with your partner is contingent on the investments you are making right now. You

determine the value of your relationship. What will your
investment be? You might have

Fear is no reason to make rash decisions or an uncalculated investment.

to start making the investment
of quality time. Or someone
will have to start making the
investment acts of service. Whatever your investment is,
make sure it's for the benefit of the relationship and not just
yourself. As with any investment, there will be a risk of loss.
One important rule of investing is to make decisions based
on calculations and not desperations. Don't make
investments in people or relationships because you're scared
of being alone. Fear is no reason to make rash decisions or
an uncalculated investment. Even Warren Buffett with all his
success has made investments and lost money, however,
with each lost, he learned from his losses. You win some and
you learn some, because even in a loss you learn something
along the way. Despite all is wealth, Buffett makes the choice
to not use his money for selfish reasons. He still lives is a
house that he bought in 1958 which then had a value of
$31,500, only a fraction of what the house is worth today.
Despite being worth billions of dollars, Warren Buffett lives
off a salary of $175,000 annually. He gives more than 90% of
his wealth to charities and foundations. In 2015, he gave 2.8
billion to the Bill and Melinda Gates foundation. Even with all
his wealth, Mr. Buffett gives a great example that the greatest

investment any one person can make is in humanity, impacting the lives of others.

What is going to be your impact in your relationship? Men, your cars can't come and say kind words at your funeral. Women, your shoes won't be able to come be at your side if you're sick. We can invest our resources in so many things that will never bring us life. But the greatest investment we can ever make can be in the life of someone else. Why not make that investment with your partner and reap the full return of your investment. Don't be like Otis Redding and have to sing a sad song:

"You don't miss your water
Till your well runs dry."

Invest in your relationship before you lose it. Establish what the relationship is worth so you know what to do to keep it.

Chapter 11

The Fight before the Fight

Tomorrow will never happen because every time it shows up, it is today...Take advantage of the moment. Fight for tomorrow by preparing today.

What would you say is the hardest sport to train for? Is it basketball? What about football? Maybe even soccer? As a former athlete, I have endured some long training hours and challenging times for the chance to compete for victory. Often, you get hurt in training and it delays the process for competition. Many people hate the training process or even practice because they want to just play the sport or game of choice. Even basketball legend, Allen Iverson, was ridiculed for his position on practice. He loved playing the game but didn't like practice. A good coach will tell you, that how you practice is how you play. You can't expect to play what you

126

have not practiced. Training is a part of the practice. What you are willing to train for is what you are willing to be a champion in. I never met a champion that was not willing to sacrifice time, resources, and effort for training. Cover Ground, a digital media platform for athletes, once asked a question. What is the hardest sport to train for? They gave a list of the top 5 sports that were the hardest to train for.

Here is that list:
- Rugby
- Track
- MMA – Mixed Marital Arts/UFC
- Gymnastics
- Wrestling

Rugby

The number five spot goes to Rugby. In a toss-up between Ruby and Soccer, Rugby beat out soccer. The dispute with rugby is because it's a nonstop running game like soccer; it requires a tremendous amount of endurance. At the same time it is a wild contact sport a lot like football. Even without pads, or equipment, the hits are still vicious, but the truth still lies in the fact that you need to be able to take a person running full speed into you and keep going... all while topping that with exceptional endurance level.

Track

From the outside in, all running track means to people is putting on your running shoes and running in circles. In reality, sometimes that's the hardest part of the sport. Can you run around in circles day in and out for 9 or 10 months at max velocity? Track is a sport of being 100% every time you step out to compete or you lose. Usain Bolt doesn't step on the track at 60% to try and hit his top speed.

Why field events don't make the cut with track is for one reason only... the ability for a second chance. As a field athlete, you have a minimum of three chances to make something happen. So if you mess up the first time you know you have the ability to bounce back. (With the shot at another three attempts if you make the final rounds.) On the track, you only have one chance to make it happen. Take the 100 meter dash for example; you train weeks and months for ten seconds of your life. If you mess up, it is practically over.

Mixed Martial Arts/UFC

The only reason this sport is not number one is because the training is not as insane as the actual competitions. Don't get it wrong, it's still hard, but when the bell goes in the octagon, it's a different world! And the recovery time from matches is months! With this sport, many see the end result, but that is not how they train on a daily basis or they all probably would be brain dead. Nonetheless, the hours that have to go into mixed martial arts are incomparable. It is training months without end for one 3 round match. On top of all this, you can train all those hours, weeks and months and literally get knocked out in a matter of seconds; or how about a broken limb, getting your brow busted open, or taking multiple elbows in the face.

Gymnastics

Gymnastics requires sickening balance, mental toughness, body control, and even a bit of speed to get to that vault. The wipe outs in gymnastics look so painful, and never mind the fact that the injuries are some of the worst in sports. Gymnastics also carries a huge mental burden on its athletes. The goal of the sport is perfection! Every routine an athlete steps into, they are trying their best to not make a mistake. If they make a big mistake or a small infraction, there is no reset button the routine must go on. It's a team sport built off of every individual so no one wants to be the one to ruin it for the team. Most of the population of the world could not even do one practice of what gymnasts go through.

Wrestling

The main reason wrestling takes the number one spot is because it is one of the few sports where the training and the competitions are virtually the same thing. They go to practice and wrestle, then go to a wrestling match and do the same. Just like fighting, there are multiple aspects of the game that need to be worked on; And just like gymnastics, it is a team sports where individuals must thrive for the team as a whole. No one wants to be the one to blow it for the team.

Wrestling requires a crucial amount of time doing all types of crazy things...it's not just on the mat at practice. They have to get in the sauna constantly to cut weight, ice bath from the neck down because their whole body is mashed up, and refill fluids to the astonishing amount of sweat lost during wrestling.

Wrestlers along with MMA athletes are some of the toughest athletes. They do not feel pain and fight through everything that is humanly possible to fight through.

Jake Herbert a 2x NCAA Champion, NCAA career record of 149-4, Hodge Trophy winner, World Silver medal, freestyle wrestler of the year award once described his training to a report as development. Jake said, "There are three components of wrestling—physical development, technical development, and mental development—and you need to be elite in all three to be a high level wrestler". Though wrestling is a team sport, you're judged by your individual match as well. One wrestler may win a match, but the team could still end up losing.

That sounds a lot like a relationship. Often in a relationship people try to win in arguments, but end up losing the relationship. Some times when a relationship is going down, and it looks like the relationship is almost over, one partner may have the tendency to want to begin fighting for the relationship because they feel the relationship is slipping away. The fight for a relationship doesn't start when it's almost over, it starts the moment the relationship begins. When you talk to champions from various sports including wresting, those champions envisioned themselves winning while in training before the event ever started. How does this compare to a relationship?

Most athletes' training systems consist of at least two components:

- Conditioning
- Discipline

Conditioning can be defined: "as a process of changing and training behavior by rewarding or punishing a subject each time an action is performed until the subject associates the action with pleasure or distress". When you are going through conditioning, you are training your body or mind to respond a certain way. Pat Riley, former NBA player, coach and now executive for the Miami Heat was known for his strenuous practices and training. His philosophy was to put the body through a rigorous workout in practice so that when time for the game came, the body was conditioned to respond. It was ready to kick it into high gear when needed, and the body responded because it was used to the conditioning. If that applies for the body and mind of athletes; how would that apply to a relationship?

Carl and Eva were headed to divorce court. Throughout their time together, they had experienced a series of challenges within the relationship. Most of the problems were complications where issues were carried over from their time of dating. While dating, they choose to ignore these issues that were now sending them to divorce court. Eva would make suggestions that they needed counseling but Carl would brush it off and think that things would just get better over the course of time. When Eva filed for divorce, Carl was willing to go to counseling in an effort to save his marriage. Eva agreed to pause the divorce proceedings while they were in counseling. While in counseling, Eva explained to their therapist her discontent with her marriage; she felt unappreciated, undervalued, neglected and that Carl was very selfish in their marriage. After a few sessions in counseling, Carl was able to recognize the error of his ways. He then committed to changing and trying to do things better and be a better husband. After a few weeks of this commitment, Carl went back to his old ways and was just as selfish as before. Tired and frustrated Eva followed through with her plans for a divorce. Carl could not understand, why things fell apart. Carl felt that he was willing to fight for his marriage but couldn't understand why things weren't working for him. The reason things fell apart was because Carl was never conditioned for the fight from the start. You cannot perform what you have never practiced. Fighting for a relationship is not something you turn on and turn off whenever you get ready. One must condition himself to do the things to maintain a relationship before a relationship needs repair. Carl was ready to fight but lacked the endurance that the fight really needed. If Eva felt unappreciated, undervalued and neglected, Carl should have been practicing appreciating her, valuing her and paying attention to her. The same way athletes must condition themselves to compete in an event, a person must condition himself to do the things that makes that relationship work. You fight for the relationship every day before challenging times appear.

Chapter 12

Deliberate Love – Loving on Purpose

Everything you want is outside your comfort zone

What is Love?

What is your love's measuring stick?

What defines love?

Is it a feeling?

Is it an emotion?

Does love just happen; does it choose us unknowingly?

Can we choose who we fall in love with?

Is fallen in love realistic?

Does love last forever?

How do we know that we are in love?

These were the questions swirling around in my head when I was writing this chapter.

These are all valid questions as it pertains to love. When we think about relationships, love is typically the goal, the status quo or reason why we are in a relationship. It's human nature to seek out love and desire love. Some people are in love with being in love, but have never really loved. If you Google or look up the meaning of love, so many things come up. Our society defines love in a variety of ways. Before we get into what our society thinks, let's go back a little. I believe that humans are by design. The way our bodies work and maneuver there has be to a designer to the creation we call a body. The functions in our body all serve a purpose. How our hands are designed to hold things. How our nose is connected to our mouth and we can smell things and imagine how it taste. What about how the skin on the bottom of your feet is different from the other skin on your body. All of that is by design and is for a reason. If that is true to the physical part of who we are; what about the emotional part of who you are? I believe love has a standard. The question is what is your standard? Do you base love on what you see on television and movies? Is your view of love based on your social media feed and the opinions that you see there? Is it based on what you saw in your home growing up? Many people did not grow up in a loving home so their view of what love is and should be is polluted and colored with bad experiences and unhealthy examples. I believe love is by design. If your body has a designer so does your emotions. In writing this book, I wanted to appeal to a variety of audiences. This book is not just for women; it's for men as well. This book isn't a written from a religious perspective, even though I am a licensed minister. I didn't write this book to impose my personal views as a born again believer. However, in writing this section, I wanted a standard from a source that has been in existence longer than any other source of information that I have come across. I chose to use the Holy Bible and a passage that talks about love. In addition, weather you are religious or not, the bible is a book of principles and experiences that have been shared for generations. The passage I would like to use as a reference/standard is found in the New Testament, 1 Corinthians Chapter 13, verses 4-7. Here is what is says from the New Living Translation:

4, Love is patient and kind. Love is not jealous or boastful or proud **5,** or rude. It does not demand its own way. It is not irritable, and it keeps no record of being wronged. **6,** It does not rejoice about injustice but rejoices whenever the truth wins out. **7,** Love never gives up, never loses faith, is always hopeful, and endures through every circumstance.

From these few lines of this passage, we can some up the definition of love as:

Selfless thoughts, words and behavior towards another, having their best interest in mind.

In order to do that, love is not something that just happens, it has to be a conscience choice. In a new relationship, love can be confused with infatuation. Love is more than how sexy a person is, it's about how selfless a person is.

Let's break down this passage. Everything that is stated is something that has to be done by choice. If you didn't choose it and you say it just happened then the question is, "is it love?" You meet someone, sparks start to fly and you guys get hot and heavy fast. That's not love, that's lust or infatuation. You don't love that person, you're lusting for that person. The only person you're loving at that moment is yourself because of the selfish lustful desires that you are trying to satisfy. You meet someone and you guys like being around each other and you feel like you can't go a day without seeing each other but each time you get together, things end up in an argument. Is

Love is more than how sexy a person is, it's about how selfless a person is.

137

that love? If you can't communicate without insult; someone is putting his or her needs ahead of the other. So ask yourself. Is that Love? In order to love, in order to experience love, it has to come from a selfless place. Look at the first line is this passage.

Love is patient and kind.

Wow, patience and kindness alone are obstacles in many relationships. Sometimes it seems like after a period of time with a person and in a relationship, the kindness and patience go right out the door. You're rushing them to get ready; you say something insulting or mean to them, why? Because you're in a rush and you lash out at your partner. Are you choosing to act in a loving manner at that moment? Not at all. Let's continue to see what else the passage says.

Love is not jealous or boastful or proud or rude.

Jealousy, boasting, pride and rudeness. Think for a second how many relationship you know of, including the relationships you have been in, are riddled with this type of behavior and treatment. But all the while, saying that they are in a loving relationship. This goes back to my point of having proper examples of what love is. In preparation for

138

this book, I had the pleasure of meeting and interviewing hundreds of couples. I remember one couple, where the male said he knew that his women loved him when she searched through his phone. He was mistaking her jealousy, for love. That was funny and sad in hearing that comment from that young man. Funny because I have seen and experienced that type of behavior; sad because that's his measuring stick for love in his relationship.

In the movie "Get on Up", a biopic of the entertainer James Brown, there was a scene that depicted James Brown's parents and the type of relationship they had. In one scene, James' father comes home, his mother confronts him and questions him because he has been gone for a long time. The two exchange words and James' father begins to rough up his mother. The mother picks up a pot and throws it at the father. The father then rushes her and begins to rough her up even more. All the while, James Brown a little boy is watching this scene unfold. In a split second, the couple goes from a violent exchange into a warm embrace and begin to kiss each other and then passionately kiss and hug and.... Well the scene changes and we are left to imagine what happens next, more than likely a sexual exchange between his parents. With little James Brown seeing this exchange, he is learning this behavior by observation. Fast forward in the

139

movie when James Brown is married to his first wife. He has

Don't ask why someone keeps hurting you; ask why you keep letting them

a heated verbal exchange with his wife about not answering the phone when he called her the day before. When it looked like things were about to get physically violent, the two begin to kiss and embrace each other romantically. This behavior was learned. More than it being learned, it was his example of what love was. Love is not about being rude, jealous or physically violent to one another. If you have experienced this type of treatment, I want to let you know; that is not love its abuse. In addition; abuse can be verbal or physical. Don't ask why someone keeps hurting you; ask why you keep letting them. Love shouldn't hurt it should heal.

It does not demand its own way

The first word we said in the definition of the word love was "selfless". Many of us have learned to care for things and people from a selfish place. Everything is all about you. It's always about how you feel, what's in it for you. That's what I call the "Ish." The Ish is all about you. The "Less" is about the other people around you. Ish vs. Less. In order to really love, we have to start from a "less" place. Over the course of a relationship, many challenges and unforeseen issues will

140

arise. When resolving issues and challenges, the mindset should be from a "less" place. The "less" is interested in a win win situation. The solution that is devised will create an environment where both parties can win. The "ish" will have the mindset of how can I win. Often we find selfless people with selfish people and there is a tug of war going on. One party feels that they are giving more than the other party and it

Love shouldn't hurt it should heal.

creates an unbalance in the relationship and usually an unhappy situation. So how do we create balance and a selfless environment in a relationship? St. Francis Assisi was remembered for these words, "All getting separates you from others, and all giving unites to others." As with creating any realm of change, the change must first begin within the mind first. When I talked to couples where one person was being accused of being selfish; the person that was selfish was typically scared of what they might lose in the process of giving. The fear of losing trapped them into being selfish. They hated to lose, therefore, felt they needed to win. Also, many of the persons I talked to grew up in an environment that if they did not look out for themselves, others around them would take advantage of them, thus losing again. Regardless of the previous situations and past experiences, this requires a change in mindset to view giving as winning.

When we go back to a team mindset, our partner should be viewed as just that; a partner and not someone of the opposite side. When in a relationship, we can sometimes take the position of opponents and not partners. If that is your view then you will always try to win against them, rather than winning with them.

Solid character will reflect itself in consistent selfless behavior, while selfish poor character will seek to hide behind deceptive actions and using others.

The next area we need to make adjustments, to create a selfless environment is our conversation. What we say is an indication of what we think. If we address our mind first, our speech should follow. Many times we say one thing but think another. Our goal should be on one accord. Saying things that build up our partner rather than tearing them down. Making a conscious effort daily to build up your partner should be your goal. One way to do this is having a daily goal of saying nice things. Take time to verbally praise your partner to create a selfless environment. Identify qualities that your partner has and magnify them. Now a goal might seem a bit strange but it's only a goal until it becomes a part of your normal behavior. Our goal is to develop the character of being selfless and having our partner's best interest in mind. Solid character will reflect

142

itself in consistent selfless behavior, while selfish poor character will seek to hide behind deceptive actions and using others.

Finally, if we are thinking correctly and speaking graciously then

Until you change your mind about what you're thinking, you will never be able to change your mind about what you are doing

our actions should fall right in line. Many times we focus on our actions before we focus on how we think and how we speak. It's hard to change what you doing if you haven't changed your mind about what you doing. Until you change your mind about what you're thinking, you will never be able to change your mind about what you are doing. Selfless actions come easier when you have selfless thoughts and words preceding them.

It is not irritable, and it keeps no record of being wronged.

Selfless actions come easier when you have selfless thoughts and words preceding them

The things two people do to each other they remember. If they stay together, it's not because they forgot, it's because they forgave. Keeping a record of everything a person has ever done to you is a crippling behavior. Ask yourself this question, what is the benefit of holding onto the past hurts that someone did to me? When you choose to be unforgiving, you're reminding yourself of what they did to you. You are actually creating a prison for yourself not to be free from the hurt.

Rachelle Friedman Chapman is a young woman who is filled with a zest for life, but she's had her share of rough times. In 2010, a month before she was going to be married to her fiancé, Chris Chapman, a freak accident left her paralyzed from the chest down. Friedman and some of her friends were attending Friedman's bachelorette party. While hanging out by the pool, Friedman's girlfriend playfully pushed her into the pool. Tragically, what was meant to be a harmless prank seriously backfired. Friedman plunged head first into the shallow end of the pool, fracturing two of her vertebrae.

When you forgive others, you are making a promise never to use their past against them.

While Friedman could have sunk into despair and depression, she chose to remain positive. Her fiancé stood by her, and they were married one year after the accident. Did Friedman forgive the friend who pushed her into the pool? The answer is "No, she did not." As Friedman herself explains, "I know this is hard to believe but I never had to forgive her because I never really blamed her. As I was lying on the side of the pool, I was worried about her." Here we see a true story of forgiveness. Rather than blaming her friend, she made the choice to never blame her and never hold anything against her. As it pertains to a relationship, this is the mindset that we must develop. I say develop because it's a process and doesn't just happen overnight. Forgiveness is a promise, not a feeling. When you forgive others, you are making a promise never to use their past against them.

It does not rejoice about injustice but rejoices whenever the truth wins out. Love never gives up, never loses faith, is always hopeful, and endures through every circumstance.

Sue and David were high school sweethearts. They married young and had four children. During this time, David completed dental school, worked hard and now had an extremely successful dental practice. But this success came at a high price. Through the years, David had developed the habit of drinking too much. Now, he spent more time with his buddies nursing a beer than being with his family. Alcohol controlled him. After years and years of dealing with David's drinking problem, Sue decided that she had had enough. She made the decision to leave David. Sue felt she had forgiven David too many times already, and he was never going to change. One night while sitting on her bed waiting for David to come home, Sue cried out and said to God. I can't take this anymore, I want to help my husband but I don't know what to do. She asked God for help and what to do? Later that night David came home with the familiar smell of liquor. As she talked to her husband and talked to God at the same time; her ability to forgive her husband for years and years of alcohol abuse became a little easier. Sue had a vision; God was right in the room with her as she talked to David. Sue stated, I guess if Jesus could die a painful death for me, and forgive me of my sins, then I can try and forgive you. I love you, but you've got to get help." David didn't change overnight. It took him one and a half years to quit drinking alcohol totally. Sue immersed herself in the Bible and talked to God constantly and kept asking God to help her see David as the man God saw, not a man troubled by his addiction. After each relapse, David would get back up and recommit himself to try again. His sincere efforts kept Sue's hope alive. Finally, after an annual fly-fishing trip with his buddies, David returned home with the usual puffy, red eyes and pale skin of the man who had too much to drink. "Sue, I can't do this on my own." David shouted. He slowly climbed the stairs to their bedroom, but instead of collapsing into a deep sleep, he knelt at the foot of the bed, laid his head down on his folded hands and wept. "Jesus," he cried out. "I can't change. I need your help. I need you in my life, please help me beat my alcoholism." Unexplainably, a sense of peace and calm swept over David. He looked around and didn't see anything yet he felt a power surge through him, giving him the strength to change. Filled with hope, he went downstairs to tell Sue about his supernatural experience. "Sue, I committed my life to Christ just now and asked him to help me never drink another drop of alcohol. I can't explain it but I felt like He was in the room with me. I know I can change, I can beat my alcoholism." Sue cried as she hugged David. Together, they started over. They made new friends and fell in love with each other all over again. David never drank another drop of alcohol. But there was still one more thing Sue didn't know – one more secret requiring her absolute forgiveness. While driving to the mountains for a romantic weekend alone, David knew he had to tell Sue about a one-time affair he had during a drunken binge. When they arrived at the cabin, David, with trembling hands, turned off the car's ignition. He couldn't look at Sue for a long moment; then, finally, he faced her and, with his eyes filled with tears, softly said, "Sue, I have a confession to make. I've asked God for forgiveness, but I never thought I should ask you. One time when I was drunk I slept with another woman. I am sorry. I was so drunk and it only happened one time. Can you forgive me for this?" Stunned, Sue was speechless. *Lord, what do I do now? How do I handle this?* "David, I don't know what to say…. I need to be alone." Tears streaming down her cheeks, she grabbed her Bible, hiked up the mountainside and sat on a secluded rock. "God, I feel so hurt and dishonored. How could he do this to me? How many times do I have to forgive this man?" All alone, she cried out to God for hours. Again she felt God tell her that she should forgive David just as Christ had forgiven her. Sue climbed down off that rock and went to find David in the cabin. "David, I'm hurt beyond words. I didn't think I could forgive you of this, but with God's help I will try," she said. The hurt took time to heal. Although Sue had said she forgave David but the pain and emotions would creep up and threaten to discourage her. During these times she determined to not allow her mind to dwell on the pain. Whenever thoughts about David and his betrayal against her entered her mind, she would imagine Jesus standing at a chalkboard with junk scribbled all over it. Then Jesus would take an eraser and erase all the junk, making the chalkboard completely clean. Sue focused on the clean slate and kept reminding herself that the eraser had done its work. Gradually, her hurt feelings faded, and were replaced with feelings of love and commitment. Thirty years later, David still hasn't tasted a drop of alcohol. Sue and David have an effervescent marriage. They work together in his dental practice and counsel married couples in their church. On a scale of 1 to 10, Sue says their marriage is a 15. This story truly depicts and embodies selfless behavior and not giving up on love. One might say Sue was unwise to stay with a man that mistreated her for all those years, but Sue mad a choice for love to prevail. True Love never gives up and never gives in. One might even say, where was David's love all those years of drinking? David's loved switched from himself and indulging in addictive behavior to the love of God and then, he was able to properly love his wife. Thirty years later they are still choosing to love each other whole-heartedly. Love is more than a feeling. Love is not a destination to hope for, it's a journey to live through.

Love recognizes no barriers. It jumps hurdles, leaps fences, and penetrates walls to arrive at its destination full of hope – Mayo Angelou

We must make the choice to love deliberately. Get in the L.O.O.P. Love on optimal purpose.

Chapter 13

Audio Technician

Listening is a gift that requires attention over talent, spirit of ego, others over self

Susan and Aaron have been courting each other for approximately 6 months. They are in a committed relationship and saw each other exclusively. They both have aspirations of marriage and look forward to a life long journey together. One day while shopping together, Susan decided to try on some clothing and get Aaron's opinion. They had only been in the mall for 10 minutes when she saw an outfit in the store window that she liked and wanted to try on. Her mind began to wonder how the outfit would look on her. She was unsure if it would complement her body type. Excited and uncertain she proceeded into the store to find her size and try some things on for Aaron. Susan took a few items to the dressing room. She took a few different sizes to see what she liked the most and fit the best. Aaron sat in the area reserved for onlookers of persons trying on outfits. This was one of their first shopping experiences together so he had no idea what he was in for. Susan stepped out the dressing room wearing first outfit. Aaron smiled as he saw her turn the corner; he liked the way she looked in it. It was a blouse and pant suit. She modeled it a little for him and they both exchanged banter and laughter. Aaron liked the outfit and thought that it was a winner. Susan returned to the dressing room and tried on another ensemble. This time when she came around the corner, she was a little hesitant. Susan was not as comfortable in this outfit as the previous one. Aaron looked at it and said he liked it, and then asked her how she felt. Susan said its ok, but she was not sure. She returned to the dressing room yet again to try on more clothing. The next outfit was a skirt set that she liked and he liked as well. Susan went back to the sale floor to see what else was available for her to look at and she returned with more outfits. As she walked past Aaron on her way to the dressing room, she smiled at him and he smiled back. Aaron really liked the first outfit she tried on and at this moment it was his favorite. By the fourth outfit, the outfits started looking alike but Aaron was still being a trooper but didn't understand what Susan was looking for exactly. While in the dressing room, Susan was having her own mental battle of her weight and how her body wasn't the same as it was in high school. Susan had put on a few pounds in the last few months and was having some issues as to why she was gaining weight. Her self-confidence was wavering. She was trying to feel better about herself and she thought a new outfit would boost her confidence. This was an internal and mental battle within Susan that Aaron had no idea she was dealing with. By the sixth ensemble, Susan was getting a little discouraged and came out the dressing room with less vigor than she did before. This time when she came out and asked Aaron "what do you think". Aaron responds "it's nice but I like the first blouse and pant suit the best". Susan just looks at Aaron with a blank stare and turns around to returns to the dressing room. Susan begins to cry while in the dressing room. She takes off the last outfit and places it on the return rack. She comes out the dressing room empty handed and tells Aaron that she is ready to go. Aaron asks, "What's wrong?" and she says "nothing." The two head home and the ride home in the car is very quiet. Susan says very little and just stares out the window while on the way home. Aaron pulls up to her place and begins to get out the car but she asked if he could just drop her off because she wanted to be alone. Confused, Aaron agrees and makes sure she gets in ok and drives off. Aaron was puzzled as to what just happened. He thought they were having a great time and couldn't understand what went wrong. While driving, a text comes to Aarons phone which reads "Why didn't you like the last outfit, do you think I'm fat...?"

 What just happened? How did a day of shopping go from great date to bad date? Susan and Aaron apparently either had a breakdown in communication or Aaron struck a nerve. I think he did both. Where was the breakdown in communication? Why did Aaron's comments have an adverse reaction from Susan? What part did Susan play in the picture? Who is to blame?

It's no secret that men and women communicate differently but if we are going to have an affective relationship, we must learn how our partner communicates.
Within a relationship, there are four conversations occurring.

- What was said
- What was heard
- What was meant
- What was felt

In the art of communication, the objective is to have all of these in agreement and alignment. There are times when you say one thing but your partner hears something totally different. There are also times when you mean one thing but your partner feels totally different from what you meant. Good communication is not hard but it's something that we have to work on constantly. Good communication is the fuel that keeps the fire of your relationship burning. Without it, your relationship can grow cold.

Aaron and Susan are having some communication issues in the early stages of their relationship. Now is a perfect time to address these issues rather than allowing them build up into something greater and getting out of hand. Communication is a two way street. Both communicator and receiver have responsibilities in a conversation. Most people don't listen with the intent of understanding, they listen with the intent of responding. How can we effectively listen when all we are thinking about is what we are going to say after they finish speaking?

Good communication is the fuel that keeps the fire of your relationship burning. Without it, your relationship can grow cold.

Looking at Aaron and Susan's situation. What happened here? In this story, there are many conversations going on, but the question is; what is being communicated. It seemed as if things started going south after a few tries of different

154

clothing. Things took a turn for the worst when Aaron made his last statement

Breaking down the conversation:

What was said:

It's nice but I like the first blouse and pant suit the best

What was heard:

I think this outfit doesn't look right, you look fat in it

What was meant:

Out of all the things I've seen you try on, the one I like the most is the first one. You looked the best in it and you seemed to like it too.

What was felt:

Aaron thinks you're unattractive. He thinks you're fat

Where was the breakdown in communication? Why did Aaron's words stir up something within Susan? Where did the heard and the felt part of the conversation come from? It came from the receiver of the information. The said and meant came from the communicator. As I said before, both communicator and receiver have responsibilities in a conversation. Was Aaron

Most people don't listen with the intent of understanding, they listen with the intent of responding

being insensitive? Did Susan have a responsibility to convey how she was feeling?

Based on my study of human behavior, I believe there are seven key responsibilities within communication. Three for the communicator (Talker); and Four for the receiver (Listener). Let's review these responsibilities.

Receiver
Lose the assumption – receiver
Listen to hear and not to respond (empathic listening)– Receiver
Listen with your partner in mind
Don't interrupt – Receiver

Communicator

Take time to explain – Communicator
Communicate with you partner in mind – Communicator
Say what you mean, mean what you say – Communicator

The receiver is the person that is listening. Within a conversation, they will have to play both roles as well. However, you can't listen and speak at the same time. Being a good listener is a valuable attribute in a relationship. The reason why it's so valuable is because true listening takes care and it shows that you care. Often in relationships, people stop listening because they stop caring. If you really want to show your partner that you care, start by listening.

Lose the Assumption

The first responsibility as a good receiver is to "Lose the assumption." Assumption is defined as a thing or thought that is accepted as true or as certain to happen but without proof. Without proof or facts, you are only making an assumption. In addition, people hear based upon how they think and how they feel.

Often in relationships, people stop listening because they stop caring. If you really want to show your partner that you care, start by listening.

If you're feeling and thinking are incorrect, then you're listening through a filter of assumption. You are not listening to what is being said, you are only listening to what you are feeling. Within a relationship, we have the tendency to listen with the filter of how we feel and what we think.

When we listen with that kind of filter, it opens the door for assumption and not assessment. When we assume, we project our own feelings and emotions into the conversation by not allowing the communicator to explain themselves or convey what they are really trying to say.

In my first marriage, I resigned from a job that cut my salary in half and wanted me to perform the same duties for less salary. While on this job, I also had my own small business. I made the decision to resign from this position and pursue my entrepreneurial career in this venture. Before I made this decision, I consulted with my

> *Within a relationship, we have the tendency to listen with the filter of how we feel and what we think*

then wife on my plans and asked her opinion of the situation. She told me to go ahead and that she would support my decision to resign. I then explained to her the conditions and why I wanted to resign. Unfortunately all she heard was that I wanted to resign. She felt that I was leaving a job to start my own business and acting irresponsible. I actually didn't find out how she felt until 2 years later when we were in a discussion regarding our marital challenges. For two years, she withheld how she felt about something, however for two years her actions towards me were filtered by how she felt about the situation. I had no idea how she felt. She did not communicate her concerns to me. She assumed that I just left the job without having an actual reason apart from wanting to strike out on my own with my own business. An assumption can be the termite of a relationship, eating away secretly and not even noticing it. When a termite eats away at wood underneath, the surface looks good but it is weak from the inside out.

Listen to hear not to respond

Are you really listening to what is being said or are you just waiting for them to finish so you can place your two cents in on the conversation? When your partner is talking, you have to understand what your partner is saying and what they are not saying as well. In order to do this, you must become an empathetic listener. Empathic listening is paying attention to the other person with empathy. Emotionally identifying, compassion, feeling and insight. You can't be empathetic if you're so ready to respond without paying attention to what they are truly saying. Pay attention to what is being said and listen for what is not being said. Empathetic listening is method that can help you accomplish good communication thus helping you avoid distracting and assaultive behaviors within your relationship. Here are some techniques on how to become an empathetic listener:

- **Be nonjudgmental** – Don't minimize or trivialize what your partner is saying to you. When you trivialize what your partner is saying, you are saying that your thinking, your feelings, your concerns are more important than your partners.

- **Ask** - Affirm your understanding by asking clarifying questions. Restate what you perceived your partner was saying.

- **Pause** – Before you answer or respond, wait and think about what they really said. Don't feel that you have to immediately respond. Sometimes if you take a moment of silence allowing your partner to get it all out, they themselves may break the silence and offer a good solution to the issue at hand.

- **Read your Partner** - Observe your partner's emotions at the time. Pay attention to body language. See if your partner is angry, afraid, frustrated or resentful; recognize the emotions as well as the words they are using.

Empathy is the heart and soul of good listening. To experience empathy, you have to place yourself in the other person's position and allow yourself to sense what it is like to your partner at that moment. This is not easy. It requires energy and awareness. But it is a generous and helpful thing to do, and it simplifies communication.

Listen with your partner in mind

"Pride is concerned with who is right, humility is concerned with what is right ". Ezra Taft Benson.

When your partner is talking, they are addressing things from their perspective. While you are listening, you are not taking into consideration what they have to say but you begin to make the conversation about your feelings and ideas. When we turn a conversation around and make it all about us, we discount and discredit the way our partner feels.

A husband was going to a party where he would be meeting his wife's coworkers from her new job for the first time. He felt restless as the time for the party grew near, and questioned whether they would like him or not. He rehearsed

> "Pride is concerned with who is right, humility is concerned with what is right."

various scenarios in his mind in which he tried in different ways to impress them. He grew more and more stressed. On the way to the party, the man came up with a completely different approach, one which caused all of his anxiety to melt completely away. He decided that, instead of trying to impress anyone, he would spend the evening simply listening to them and summarizing what they say. At the party, he spent the evening listening carefully to everyone, responding with phrases like, "I understand what you're saying, you feel strongly that. . ." and "Let me see if I understand what you mean. . ." He also avoided voicing his own opinions, even though at times, it meant biting his tongue to keep from doing so.

To his surprise, he discovered that no one noticed or commented on the fact that he was just listening. Each person he talked to during the evening seemed content to be listened to without interruption. On the way home, his wife (whom he had not told about the experiment) told him that a number of people had made a point of telling her what a remarkable person he was. The word "charismatic" was used by one person to describe him, while another said he was one of the most "articulate" people she had ever met.

What if you could change your relationship today by simply listening and paying attention to what your partner has to say? What would your world look like if you took that approach? Always making a conversation about you and what you do is a sign of selfishness. Imagine a world where people actually listened to one another, rather than just waiting for the other people to stop talking so they can give their personal opinion.

Don't Interrupt

As a child, I was taught not to interrupt people while they were talking. I was told that it was rude. I don't think that message is getting across to our present society and generation. I believe the opposite is being taught subconsciously. With reality television and talk shows leading the way, people are being taught that loud, overly aggressive, in your face communication is being condoned and almost encouraged. People are taking clues from their favorite shows and making insulting remarks. Constantly interrupting, trying to over talk or out talk people in their life or even their partner. Interruptions in a conversation sends a few messages:

- "I'm more important than you are."
- "What I have to say is more interesting, accurate or relevant."
- "I don't really care what you think."
- "I don't have time for your opinion."
- "This isn't a conversation, it's a contest, and I'm going to win."

If we are trying to create a nurturing and beautiful relationship, are these the types of messages we want to convey to our partner? Is this the environment we want for our relationships? Constant interruption in conversations devalues your partner. It hinders the process of becoming a

163

great partner. We all think and speak at a different pace. If you are a quick thinker and an agile talker, the responsibility is on you to relax your pace. When listening to someone talk about a problem, refrain from suggesting solutions, while they are talking. Often times your partner is not looking for advice, they want an ear to listen and a heart to feel what they are expressing. If they don't ask for it don't give it. . Somewhere

When you plant the seed of listening without interruption; not only are you showing your partner that you care, you will reap the harvest of them showing you the same courtesy.

down the line, if you are absolutely bursting with a marvelous solution, at least get your partner's permission. Ask, "Would you like to hear my ideas?"

Being patient with your partner while they are talking creates an understanding environment for your relationship to flourish and grow. Your partner needs you to listen without interruption. When you plant the seed of listening without interruption; not only are you showing your partner that you care, you will reap the harvest of them showing you the same courtesy.

Communicator Responsibilities

Take time to Explain

In the 2010 installment of the Karate Kid, The Karate Kid, 12-year-old Dre Parker (played by Jaden Smith) could've been the most popular kid in Detroit, but his mother's (played by Taraji P. Henson) latest career change landed him in China.. Being an unpopular new kid amongst different kids in town, Dre has an enemy of the class bully, Cheng. In the land of kung fu, Dre knows only a little karate, and Cheng puts "the karate kid" on the floor with ease. With no friends in a strange land, Dre has nowhere to turn but to the maintenance man Mr. Han (played by Jackie Chan), who is secretly a master of kung fu. When Mr. Han takes on Dre as a student, he begins with making him do a monotonous task of taking his jacket off and on. For hours and hours and even days, Dre takes his jacket off and on over and over. After being weak and tired from his monotonous task, Dre out of frustration confronts Mr. Han and tells him he's done with his training and doesn't want to learn kung fu from him anymore and these tasks are stupid. Mr. Han then confronts Dre and asks him to go through the motions of taking his jacket on and off. While going through the motions of taking is jacket on and off; Mr. Han explains what each motion means and how it plays a vital part in kung fu. Dre discovers that each motion is a movement of defense or offense in the art of kung fu. Dre didn't understand what he was doing until proper explanation was given.

In the art of communication with your partner never take for granted, they automatically understand what you are saying. Just like Dre, some of us are just going through the motions and not paying attention to what is actually going on and what is being said. A communicator in a relationship must have the objective of getting their point across to their receiver. This may take using extra words, analogies or examples in order for you and your partner to understand one another. When you are done explaining in a conversation, your partner should be confident not confused. Taking time to explain yourself shows that your personal agenda is not the main point of the relationship but that the continuity of the relationship is.

Communicate with your partner in Mind

Knowing the background and understanding the needs of your partner is key when we communicate with them in mind. Taking into consideration their feelings, their insight, their abilities, and the way they look at information. It will take practice but there is a benefit when you communicate and talk to your partner with them in mind. One way to communicate with your partner in mind is to find a common ground with whatever subject you are discussing. Rather than looking at the differences or your opinions, focus on the common things that can draw your ideas together. Using phrases like:

- I understand what you're saying, I feel the same
- I can see how you feel like that
- You have a valid point and I can appreciate that view

These phrases can connect us and be pathways to showing understanding for your partner.

Imagine it this way. Let's say you are stuck on an island with only one other person. This person only speaks another language while you only speak English. In order for you guys to communicate with one another effectively, you can't continue speaking your language to them and they can't continue speaking theirs to you. Someone is going to have to take the initiative to learn the other person's language. You will only frustrate yourself trying to talk to them in your language and they will be frustrated because they don't understand you. Take time to understand and learn the language of your partner. The easiest way to cause a misunderstanding is to treat your partner like they already understood.

Say what you mean, mean what you say

Why are there so many misunderstandings in a relationship? You meet someone and everything is going great until you have that first misunderstanding and it seems like from there, things begin to go south sometime. Most misunderstandings stem from miscommunication and not

> The easiest way to cause a misunderstanding is to treat your partner like they already understood.

understanding what was really said. Joking and being jovial can sometimes backfire when we converse with our partner causing a trail of miscommunication. As a jovial person I have to make sure, I am sensitive to the subject when I am talking to my partner. In regular everyday conversation, joking and playing around may not hurt anyone's feelings but on more serious subjects, putting away your joking hat may prove to be best.

Sometimes we hear phrases like: "I was only playing with you" or "Just kidding". There is a time and place for all things and you will have to play it by ear to find out when is a good time to play and joke with your partner.

One way to cut down on some of our misunderstandings is to say what we mean and mean what we say. I call it the three C's of communication:

- Be Clear
- Be Concrete

- Be Courteous

Be Clear - When you want to deliver a point in a conversation, the first thing you want to be is clear. Lose vague or ambiguous information. Stay focused on the main objective of the conversation. Ask yourself, "What is the purpose of this conversation?" Stay on that purpose and try not to sway or be swayed. To be clear, try to minimize the number of ideas you are conveying. People shouldn't have to "read between the lines" and make assumptions on their own to understand what you're trying to say.

Be concrete – When you're speaking with your partner, you must be concrete. The receiver should have a clear picture of what you are trying to say. Words create images and pictures in the mind of your partner. Are your words painting Picassos or are your words painted by a two year old at home on a kitchen counter with a box a crayons. To be concrete, stay with the facts and make sure you have details. Unfortunately, men and women sometimes communicate differently. Men have a tendency to leave out details and get to the end of a story quickly; while women can take you on a journey with their words and you may wonder what the actual point to the story. Learning how you partner likes to communicate is part of the process in communication. You can't always expect your partner to understand you when

169

you haven't taken the time to understand them. This communication has to be a two way street between both parties. Staying away from sarcasm is a great way to be concrete in your communication. Sarcasm can create distance between you and you partner.

Be Courteous

Courteous conversation is kind, open, and truthful. There are ways to say truthful things without damaging or hurting your partner's feelings. Your communication should not include hidden insults or passive aggressive tones. Keep in mind you want to communicate with your partner in mind. Even when you're communicating with something that involves you, still think about how your partner will feel and think with the information that you are expressing. When relationships are fresh and new, people have the propensity to be very courteous but overtime, something happens and we get used to that person and think that courtesy is something that we don't have to focus on. Regardless of the stage in your relationship, if you have been together for three months, three years or three decades, courtesy will take you farther than being insulting or malicious in your communication.

Remember Aaron and Susan? Knowing what we know now,

let's look how and what happened in their communication. Like we said both communicator and receiver have responsibilities. What should have happen with Aaron and Susan? Susan should have been more open to share about what was going on with her internal battle of body image issues. That may have given Aaron insight and sensitivity with this situation; instead he was just in the dark and didn't know how to handle the issue. When Susan was the receiver, she made an assumption about Aaron's statement. Making an assumption can only cause more confusion within your communication thus causing damage in the long run. Aaron should have taken time to explain his statement as well. Aaron also didn't communicate with his partner in mind by understanding the sensitive issue of a women's weight and body image issues. Paying closer attention to what you say in your relationships will open us up to being sensitive to our partner's needs and desires within the relationship. If Aaron and Susan follow some of these guidelines of communication, they should be fine. After looking at some of these guidelines, how is your communication with your relationship? Are you being a responsible communicator? Are you being a responsible receiver? There will always be an area with in a relationship that we will need to work on. Communication is the lubricant to a healthy relationship; but being misunderstood can be a cancer waiting to spread into

171

other areas of your relationship. Take time to learn your responsibilities as a communicator and receiver in your relationship. Men, women don't always want you to fix every problem they come to you with, sometimes they just want to be heard. Women, men won't automatically understand everything you say, take time to explain not only what you are saying but also what you are feeling.

Chapter 14

No Plan B

Interest may get you started but commitment is what keeps you going

In February of 1519, a very ambitious young man, named Hernan Cortes set course for a trip to Mexico. The goal of his trip was to acquire riches & wealth for Spain and fame & glory for himself. Hernan's ambition always set him apart from his peers. He was elected captain for the expedition to Mexico at the age of 34, in time where captains were usually older. Cortes thirst and hunger for power and fame drove him to extreme measures. He partially funded the expedition to Mexico with his own money, because he refused to lose. When the governor of Cuba recalled the mission to Mexico and revoked Hernan's charter; Hernan ignored his orders and set sail for the adventures to the mainland. All his life, he wanted to make a name for himself and he was not about to let the opportunity slip away from him. He was determined to accomplish the goals that he had set for himself and refused to let anyone stand in his way. With 11 ships, 500 men, 13 horses and a small number of cannons Cortes landed in the new world via Mexico. Due to his arrogance and disobeying the orders of the governor, his crew began talks of mutiny and return to Cuba with Cortes' ships. Cortes refusing to lose, he burned all his ships thus sealing their fate to be committed to the mission. Hernan removed his crew's option of returning to Cuba. When he removed their option, they were forced to commit.

In our current society, it seems to be common practice to juggle more than one person at a time for a relationship. Men have a tendency to try to date more than one woman at a time, trying to figure which one is good for them. Some do this with the hopes of finding that right one. Others do it because they are greedy. I call it the F5 Syndrome. On a PC, the F5 button refreshes and updates the browser and other applications. With a man, he refreshes when he may grow tired of one female and moves to the next; or try's to juggle them all at the same time. F5 stands for the 5 types of women a man may have in his rotation/life.

1. Friend
2. Flirt
3. Fun
4. Freak

5. Fund

Typically a man tries to find all these attributes in one women. However, if he can't he will juggle these five types at any given time, based on his needs at that time.

Friend – This is a young lady that is a true friend. Someone he can have a great time with. She is typically low maintenance. He can talk to her about anything. She has probably known him for some time.

Flirt – This female is one that shares flirtatious banter between the two of them. He may be just waiting for the chance for her to take him serious. More than likely he works with her. She flirts back but doesn't follow through with her flirts.

Fun – Someone he has fun with all the time. She laughs at all his jokes. She makes him feel like he is the funniest man in the world. She plays video games, she likes sports, and she goes to concerts and loves hanging with him.

Freak – This young lady is always and readily available for physical interaction. Need I say more...?

Fund – This is the female that if he were ever to fall on hard times, she would be able to assist him financially.

This is my explanation of how several men juggle women based on their needs. He would like to have all these qualities in one woman however they rarely find it. Because of that, he feels that he is justified in his actions because no one person would be able to satisfy all these at once. He continues to juggle, always exercising his options, never really committing to one person. Many times some men look for an excuse or reason to have more than one woman. He searches for flaws and imperfections within a woman to justify not committing. He won't tell her, he will just keep her on the rotation until he can find someone to replace her.

The female gender has a tendency to want commitment; however in our current society, women have become much more like men and trying to juggle as well. The female juggle is a little different. Females typically don't like juggle men simultaneously. They have more of a trial bases for their juggle. They will try a man out for a period of time and then put that man on hold until he messes up or until someone more appealing comes into the picture. Don't be misled; there are some women that do juggle simultaneously, however, like I said it's not typical behavior. The five types of men that a female may encounter in her lifetime are the L5.

1. Leader
2. Loyal
3. Lover
4. Lender
5. Legend

Once again human nature would try to find all the attributes in one person, however that's highly unlikely. We have a tendency to try to have a Frankenstein type of mentality. We try to take one attribute from each person and create the perfect person. Wishing we could match Mike's Ambition, with John's sense of humor, with Phillips smile. Etc.

Leader – One who is a natural leader and is gifted in the area of leadership. He has an entrepreneur type for a mind. She would follow him anywhere because she trust in his ability to lead. He's a great conversationalist. She can talk to him about a variety of subjects because of his wealth of knowledge.

Loyal – The guy that if she were stuck on the side of the road at 3am, he would be there in a hurry no question asked. He would be there in the tough times. He was there when some other guy broke her heart, but she may not see him that way for a relationship.

Lover – The man she can always count on to give her the physical attention she needs and desires.

Lender – The man that is willing to pay her bills but may want something in exchange; her time or her touch. Or he may be the man that doesn't want anything in return but just wants to be a nice guy.

Legend – One who has a great reputation. His name precedes him. This is typically found with younger women that have heard about how great a guy is and wants him because she wants to know for herself if what she heard is true. He is legendary.

When it comes to engaging in new relationships, this has become common practice for both males and females. Some wanting to keep their options open; others wanting to be greedy never wanting to commit. Here is the thing about committing; it requires no plan B. Commitment is just that, the act of being committed. It's hard to be committed when you're looking to exercise your options. The difference between interest and commitment is; when you're interested in doing something, you do it only when it is convenient. When you're committed to something, you accept no excuses, only results. The longer we stay on the fence about something or someone, the harder it will be to commit. Time and people are precious and valuable commodities. Why waste someone's time if you're not really interested. That is just selfish behavior. We can lose money and get it back, we can lose things and replace them. But time and people are two things if lost, you can't replace. Don't waste a person's time if you have no intention on being committed to them. Bob Marley was recorded for saying, "The biggest coward of a man is to awaken the love of a woman without the intention of loving her". This goes both for males and females in this day and time. When you find someone special, have No Plan B. The moment you have an option is the moment you have the tendency to take an option. Commitment is a key component to building a strong and valued relationship. If you find yourself as someone's option, go ahead and make the choice for them. You are not a second option; either they choose you or they lose you.

In the story of Hernan Cortes, he removed the option for his crew of returning to Cuba and they were forced to stay committed to the mission at hand. You can't force anyone to choose you, but you can make him or her wish they had.

Chapter 15

Beyond the Body

People are like Oreos, the good stuff is on their inside.

In every chapter of this book, my goal is to bring the reader one step closer to having a disgustingly beautiful relationship with their future partner or current relationship. In the single section, we talked about looking beyond the body. I reviewed some fairy tales that had great moral lessons and painted a picture of how important it was to look beyond the body when looking for and waiting for a mate. Fairy tales may tell a great story however in this section, I felt the need to address the matter of looking beyond the body again from the standpoint of a current relationship. In fact, we will address the topic again in the marriage section of this book. Only in this section and the marriage section I will use actual live examples and people.

Image and physical appearance have become trivial topics of discussion for many relationships. When you meet someone one-way but they change physically over the course of time. That can really put a lot of pressure on a person and the relationship. If you meet someone and they are a certain size; if they were to change physically, would your attraction change? What if you were in a relationship and your partner suffered an injury that left them physically challenged; would that change how you feel about them? Just as relationships are filled with potentials, they are also filled with uncertainties. It's in our human nature to try to control everything that happens to us. No one can control how and if a person changes physically however you can control your response to the change.

One of the couples I interviewed for this chapter was Alex and Danielle. When I met Alex, he was sitting down and Danielle was walking up behind him preparing to greet me. They were an attractive couple together. Alex had sandy blonde hair with a short cut and broad shoulders. Danielle was a brunette with glasses and a lovely smile. Danielle hugged Alex from behind and kissed him on the cheek. They were a very affectionate couple. Danielle sat down and we began to talk about what I was doing for my book. It quickly became clear that I was going to use them for my research however not for the reason I had originally intended. I soon found out that Alex was paralyzed from the waist down. This couple had been together for under a year but they were clearly a great team together. Danielle actually was interested in one of Alex's friends but Alex proved to be a better companion for her. She looked beyond Alex's physical limitations and looked at his heart. I know there are many women out there that would not have even given Alex a chance because of his physical challenges but Danielle did. Confucius said it this way, "everything has beauty, but not everyone will see it." Are you looking for the beauty in the person's heart or just in their body and physical appearance?

As a young man, I made physical beauty, size and weight a major factor if I was going to be attracted to a woman or not. This thinking even affected my previous marriage. My views affected my marriage in a negative aspect and proved to be a challenge that my marriage faced. I learned that real beauty didn't come from the outside in; it comes from the inside out. I learned this by reevaluating what is important in a relationship. The body will change but a person's heart and values will last longer than their body. A person's size, weight or physical abilities wouldn't take care of me if I got sick. It would be that person's heart. For years, I thought that men were more visually stimulated than women;

however in my research for this book, I found many studies showing that men and women are both visually stimulated creatures. Even with both men and women being visual stimulated creatures, there is still more pressure on a woman being physically appealing. There is this pressure on women to uphold an unrealistic standard of beauty. In today's society, many women are stressed to uphold this standard of beauty. There is pressure everywhere; in movies, TV, social media, print media etc. A women's identity is not found in the pages of a magazine but it is found within her and how she chooses to define herself. I remember seeing a post on social media, it read:

A women's identity is not found in the pages of a magazine but it is found within her and how she chooses to define herself

"So you want her to be a beauty queen
with a PHD, have a big but and flat stomach
be Betty Crocker, an erotic lover in the bedroom,
and a nurse...... But you can't change a
tire, you don't have a job, your hairline is
receding & you can't defend her?
You can't ask for a complete package
If you're an empty envelope"

183

The post was funny however it exposed light on how many men think and desire for their women to be. They set impractical expectations on their partner while they barely have anything to offer. Men, your penis makes you a male but your wisdom and character makes you a man. Practice using wisdom and character to prove your manhood.

In the chapter "Deliberate Love," I told the story of Rachelle Chapman and how she was able to forgive her friends of a freak accident that left her paralyzed. However, that story has another side to it. What about her fiancé, Chris Chapman? He made the choice to stay with Rachelle and marry her in spite of her physical challenge that she endured. That says so much about his value system and his character as a human

True beauty is not in the face or the body but beauty is found in the light of a person's heart.

being. Many people would have walked away from that situation and relationship. They would have made excuses and taken a selfish route of how the injury would affect them not thinking about how their partner would have felt. It is important for me to say that physical attraction and body image do play a part in the relationship process but it is not the main thing. Our society has become fascinated with body image, beauty and shapes to an extent that it is shaping the thinking of many people. They are allowing social media and magazine etc. to tell them what beauty is. True beauty is not in the face or the body but beauty is found in the light of a person's heart.

True love is found beyond the body.

Section 3:
Marriage what's it all about?
Weddings are starting blocks not finish
lines...

Chapter 16

Maintenance is Cheaper than Repair

Extra read all about it... results happen when you do something.... not talking about it or thinking about it!!

I can remember the first car I bought from a dealership. It was a fairly new car, just two years old but it was really in a great condition. I took the car for a test drive and it rode very nice. I didn't listen to the radio while I was driving so I could listen to the engine. I rode with the salesman and he pointed out several features of the car and how the car had passed all its points of inspection with the dealer and mechanics at the shop. After the test drive, we pulled back into the dealership parking lot. I walked around the car for a last look at the car. I entered the passenger side of the vehicle and looked in the glove compartment. In the glove compartment was the owner's manual. I looked in the manual to learn more about the car and its features. At the back of the owner's manual was some information from the previous owner. It was a two-column sheet. On one side was a list of dates and maintenance on the car. On the other side was a list of repairs that he made to the car. The maintenance list was much longer than the repair side. When I brought this to the attention of the salesman, he said "maintenance is always cheaper than repairs." I understood what he was saying for the car but it wasn't until I began writing this book that this applies to marriage as well.

Rather than waiting to repair a marriage, the key is to maintain it.

In the dating section of the book, we talked about "The fight before the fight." In that section, we talked about how when a dating relationship is going down and it looks like the relationship is almost over, one partner has a tendency to want to begin fighting for the relationship. One partner may feel the relationship is slipping away and wants to fight hard for it. The fight for a relationship doesn't start when it's almost over, it starts the moment the relationship begins. You fight for the relationship every day before challenging times appear. This principle holds to be true in marriage as well. Rather than waiting to repair a marriage, the key is to maintain it.

What does maintenance look like for a marriage? The answer will be different for each marriage, however maintenance is a must. A husband and wife must communicate with each other their needs to help maintain their marriage. Spouses are not mind readers therefore talking to your partner about your needs should be an ongoing conversation. Just like when I opened the owner's manual of my car, the maintenance of the car was an ongoing thing not just a one-time thing. His maintenance helped keep the needs for repairs down on his car. Maintenance in your marriage will help you keep the repairs down in your marriage. In the Huffington Post, there was an article by Brittany Wong, Divorce Editor. In the article, they interviewed divorce lawyers and marriage therapist. From this interview, they listed nine things that should never be said in a marriage. I want to take a look at these nine things and talk about some dos and don'ts of maintenance in your marriage. Here are the nine things that should not be said in a marriage and the reason why you shouldn't say them:

1. **"You're being ridiculous"** – When you make this type of statement, you're just saying that your partner's feelings, thoughts and views don't matter. When this type of statement is made you dismiss your spouse's perspective.

What you should say instead

Instead of dismissing your spouse's feelings try to understand them by asking questions as to why they feel the way they do and ask for help in understanding their views and their side of the story.

2. **"I don't care anymore"** - Saying you don't care anymore says that you have checked out and are disinterested with the actions of your spouse. This is very dangerous. Even if it's an issue that has been going on for a while you still have the desire to bring resolve.

What you should say instead

Explain how the situation or issue is wearing you down. Let your spouse know the importance of how this issue affects the overall relationship and why this matter is so important to you.

3. **"You never" or "You Always"** - These are what you call absolutes. Saying they never do something or they always do something is very extreme. In a challenging situation, it may feel or seem like they never do something but these words are detrimental

to a marriage. This is an attack on your spouse's character and when a person is attacked, they will either shut down or retaliate. If your spouse chooses one of those options nothing will get solved because the focus is on winning the argument and not resolving the issue.

What you should say instead

Focus on the matter at hand. Try to use examples of when that issue came up and give details why and how it made you feel when your partner did what they did.

4. **"If you hadn't _____; I wouldn't**

_____" – You can fill in the blank with whatever you want, but blaming your spouse for your response is just going to provoke an argument of some sort. Don't blame your partner for your actions. You are in control of you. They are not your puppet masters and you are not their puppet.

What you should say instead

 Explain what you are feeling when they do something you don't like. "I feel _____ when you do _____. I don't want to feel that way. What adjustments can we make to fix this?"

5. **Nothing at all** – Shut down mood. Danger, Danger, Danger!!!!! If you are not talking then we have a major problem. Communication is like the oil in your car. When it's there things can flow easily, but if it's not, the engine will come to a grinding halt. Giving each other the silent treatment provides the atmosphere for misunderstandings and stops the process of resolving any issues you may face.

    What you should say instead
    You may have to take a break but don't stop talking. If you are too angry or if an issue is too hurtful, write your feelings down. Express yourself on paper or via email but don't shut down. Nothing will be solved that way

6. **"I don't need to tell you where I've been"** – There shouldn't be any need for secrecy when it comes to the whereabouts of a spouse. Unless you're planning a surprise party for them. Understand that being transparent with your spouse builds accountability and trust within your marriage. It's not about them

knowing your every move, it's about being clear and honest with your spouse.

What you should say instead

Sharing your location or plans of the day builds trust in a relationship. Saying things like "Hey after work I stopped by at the gym." Wherever it may be, clear communication is the answer.

7. **"Why can't you be more like..."** - When we make comparison we devalue our spouses. You should never compare your spouse to a previous partner or relationship. In addition, it doesn't have to be from a former partner it could be comparing a friend's spouse or a friend's relationship. Regardless of who it is, no man or women wants to be compared to another person.

What you should say instead

Take time to show appreciation for what you love about your spouse. The grass is not always greener on the other side of the fence. Sometimes you just have to water your own grass and it will grow.

8. **"I wish I never met you"** - Few phrases are more shattering than this one. This is a very hurtful statement and implies that your spouse is the blame for all your troubles. It tells them that the bad outweighs the good and all the bad is their fault.

    What you should say instead
    Before we play the blame game, consider all the factors for your challenges and how you played a role. As a married couple you are a team. If the team wins the glory is shared, if we lose then we must comfort each other to prepare for the next victorious battle. You never lose, you just learn how not to do something for the next time.

9. **"I want a divorce"** – These words should never be used as a threat to change a spouse's behavior. If it used as threat, it can ruin a marriage that may already be on shaky ice. If you don't want to split up, these words should never come out your mouth. Many marriages have a "no divorce" policy. Don't chip away at the foundation of your marriage by saying words to threaten your spouse.

What you should say instead

Don't talk out of anger. Take a break and clear your head. Make every effort to resolve any issue and stay focused. Seek professional counseling to get a clear picture of what the issues are and how they can be fixed.

I have seen how these types of statements can have a tragic effect on a marriage. Staying away from these statements is clear maintenance rather than trying to fix a problem after it happens. When a car goes in for maintenance they check all the fluids in the car to make sure everything is running properly. If a fluid is low, a mechanic will either make a recommendation for replacing the fluid or adding more. Checking fluids in a car is like checking a pulse on a person. You want to make sure that everything is at a proper rate and proper level. Just as you check a pulse on a person, you have to check the pulse of your marriage. You don't want to take anything for granted. Here are three questions you can use to check the pulse in your marriage.

1. How are you doing?
2. How am I doing?
3. How are we doing?

How are you doing?

This is a question you ask your spouse. This question is about them. You want to see how they are doing in their life. You are inquiring about them, their job, their feelings, their friends etc. You want to know what's going on with them. You are showing that you care about what they have going on outside your relationship with each other. Giving them a platform to express themselves will give you insight on how to treat them and will open the door for connection and understanding. Understanding your spouse's needs shows that you care. Remember this is not a time to make it all about you, it's a time to focus on them and their needs.

How am I doing?

When you ask this question, you are inquiring of your partner how you are doing as it pertains to the needs of them. Are you being attentive enough? Are you being selfish? Are there some things that you can do to help the relationship grow? The list could go on and on, but you get the point. This would be like asking your boss to evaluate your work. This is not done for criticism, it is done for improvement of the relationship. Asking your spouse "how am I doing" says you value their opinion and their feelings are important to you. The point of this is not to be judged but to learn how to better serve your spouse and their needs. If both partners are focused on serving the needs of the other, no one loses everyone wins.

How are we doing?

This questions focuses on the team and partnership of the marriage. There may be many components to this question. If I could paint picture of this question, the picture would be a bicycle tire. A bicycle tire is a circle, with a frame; an inner tube of rubber and an outer rubber wheel; that goes around the frame but joined and held together by spokes. You and your spouse are the inner tube and outer rubber wheel. You can only function if the spokes are strong and in good condition. This could include children, bills, communication, health, cars, etc.; all the things that happen in our life that could affect us. How we relate to these things is the "How are we doing." You have to take a step back from things and begin to evaluate how you can do things better as a team. If a spoke falls off, it affects the balance of the wheel. If several fall off the wheel won't roll. It's the same in a marriage if there are things that you don't handle well as a team, you won't roll together very well; if at all.

Checking the maintenance of your relationship will improve your marriage. Becoming one is a journey. Before taking any road trip you want to make sure your car is well maintained and it has had all its fluids checked to make sure you get to your destination safely. If you check the oil in your car for a road trip; how much more important is it to check the pulse on your marriage. Remember maintenance is always cheaper than repairs.

Chapter 17

Monuments vs. Movements

Your accomplishments of yesterday may be an enemy to your greatness for tomorrow.

While I was finishing the previous chapter, I began looking at my notes preparing myself to write this chapter. When I completed writing the chapter, I screamed out loud and said...NEXT!!!! I was anticipating completing one chapter and getting excited about starting another. A relationship can be filled with anticipation. People get excited about the first date. Some couples anticipate the first kiss. Others can't wait till they have their first walk in the park. Whatever a couple's anticipation level, a relationship is filled with moments that people look forward to. When a couple gets married, they have more moments of anticipation. The first time they make love as a married couple; the purchasing of a new home; the arrival of a new baby. All these are exciting things that happen in a married couple's life. These are also things that can happen that can pull you away from each other and create monuments and not movements. When I would talk to couples about this subject, I would hear things like; "Remember the time we went to the Bahamas?" Or I would hear something like; "We had such a great time when we had a dinner at our favorite restaurant." Statements like this may keep a couple stuck in the past monuments they have created for their relationship, but what about creating new memories and making movements. It is important for a couple to create movements. Getting stagnant in a marriage is dangerous for the longevity and strength of a couple. Creating movements in a marriage gives you something to look forward to and stimulates connection. In science, this would be kinetic energy. Kinetic energy is the energy possessed by a body because of its motion; equal to one half the mass of the body times the square of its velocity. In laymen's terms, it's energy that's in motion. If a bowling ball has kinetic energy when it is moving; when it strikes the pins some of the energy is passed on to the pins. Let's put this science principle in a marriage. When a couple is in motion creating memories, rather than looking back at memories, it transfers energy to that couple. The only time to look back as a couple is to see how far you have come.

Montell Jordan, an American songwriter, singer, and record producer was best known for his 1995 hit "This Is How We Do It." Before he was a famous singer and artiste, he was a young man that loved to attend his family's church in South Central Los Angeles. As a young artist, Montell struggled with the tug-of-war between singing and working in the church for $100 a week or going to sing in the clubs and making $300-$400 for a ten minute ballot. It was a dance club where he would meet Kristin Hudson, a young beautiful woman that caught the eye of Mr. Jordan. She was resistant to talk to him at the time but he asked her to dance. They danced for a little while and soon stopped. Kristin said his

> *The only time to look back as a couple is to see how far you have come.*

dancing was horrible and she would rather talk to him than watch him on the dance floor. The two started dating and courting each other. In the midst of their courtship, they would fall in love, while Montell's career of an R&B singer was on the rise. According to Montell, he heard that if you are a male performer in the music industry and you're not married when you enter the music business, then the likelihood of getting married becomes increasingly grim. So the two made the decision to get married in 1994. This was just a year before his hit song "This Is How We Do It" debuted. He would soon learn that being married would be a challenge whether he was in the music industry or not. Over the course of 17 years in the music industry, Montel and Kristin Jordan experienced several accomplishments and monuments in the music industry and as a couple. Kristin served as his partner and manager for several areas of his music career. They made decisions as a couple and would reap the benefits of those decisions creating a lifestyle that many would envy. Their decision to get married before his rise in the music industry was a monumental experience as a couple. As an R&B artiste he would experience a success on a major level. Montell toured with artistes like, Mary J. Blige, Boys to Men, TLC, singing to audiences of 70,000 people. Jordan once said, whether it is 7 people in the audience or 70,000, he would give the people a show. Monument after monument, Montell Jordan's career blossomed and he was a celebrity doing movies, writing songs and selling millions or albums. Throughout his success, his partner in life and partner in the music industry, Kristin was right by his side. Their union would produce four children. After 16 years in the music industry and many accomplishments, Montell was ready for something different and ready for a change. During a time of spiritual fasting, there was a tug on his heart to walk away from the music industry. As an artist and being on the road, Montell faced temptations of infidelity, alcoholism, pride and sometimes felt he had a split

202

personality. The very thing that had provided a lavish life for his family was now taking away so much from his life. He didn't know what to do. He was concerned about providing for his family that had grown accustomed to a certain lifestyle. He made a confession and prayer to God that if he left the music industry, God would have to help him accomplish it. After so many accomplishments and monuments in their career, Montell and Kristin made the decision to not live in the monuments of their past but to begin to create movements that would have a lasting effect on their marriage and others. Today, Montell and his wife Kristin serve as ministers at Victory World Church in Norcross, GA right outside Atlanta. Their marriage faced everything you could think of from disloyalty to bankruptcy. The Jordan's now help other married couples, as counselors, letting them know they can overcome any obstacle they may face in a marriage. Montell and Kristin decided not to get stuck and be stagnant in the past success and monuments of their marriage. They made the choice to make movements that would not only help them grow as a couple but also help others grow as well. Making movements and new memories in your marriage will add growth to your relationship.

Selah Moment:

As a married couple, here are a few questions that I would like for you to consider:

- What are some of your most memorable monuments as a couple?
- Are you stuck in your marriage? If so how long?
- On a scale of 1-10 how important is it for you to be unstuck?
- What is the smallest change you could make that would have the greatest impact for more movements?

Chapter 18

What's the Mission?

By becoming the answer to someone's prayer, we often find the answers to our own.

In 1988 at the rip age of 12, I would watch this show called Mission Impossible. The show was about the IMF, (Impossible Missions Force.) The show was a remake of the original series of 1966. The premise of the show was, this elite team of special government agents took impossible missions and saved the day and kept the world safe from an unknown enemy. I remember one thing that would always happen in the series. Whenever an agent would get a mission, it was via a tape recorder or audio message. The message would go over the details for the mission including; the objectives for the mission, key people involved, and any known challenges. There was one thing that was always said at the end of the message. "This message will self-destruct" in a certain number of seconds. After the message was done, the audio device would implode or start to smoke thus being destroyed. There would be no trace of the message and no way to track the information from the message. With the message gone, the agents of IMF still understood what the mission was and why they were on the mission. The question for us in this chapter is, why we want to be married and what is the mission of our marriage? We want to look at this from two perspectives.

1. If you are not married, why do you want to be married? What is your mission in marriage?
2. If you are married, have you discovered your mission in marriage? What are you doing to accomplish your mission?

The Unmarried

With interviewing various singles, dating couples and married couples for this book; I believe very few people understand why they are married and what the mission for their marriage is. Defining your mission in a marriage serves as a road map for your marriage. It gives insight and understanding on where you are going as a couple and as individuals.

In the last section of the book, I made the statement "When you know your why, your what is easier to do." Understanding your "why" shapes the choices you make, influences your decisions, and regulates the energy you put into something. I want to speak to the unmarried people first. Whether you are single, dating or engaged, you must start asking yourself some self-discovery questions. Here are just a few questions to ponder:

- Why do you really want to be married?
- What are your motives for being married?
- What individual goals do you have for your marriage?
- What goals would you have as a couple?
- What legacy would you want to leave behind as a couple?

If you are single, answering these questions honestly may help you eliminate some people in your life that don't line up with your goals. They will also help you understand if you have selfish or unselfish motives for being married. If your concept of marriage is that your partner is rescuing you from your loneliness then you are mistaken. Trust me, I know people that were married and were still lonely. Marriage does not solve loneliness. If you want to get married because you are getting older and you believe that it should have happened by now, then you may want to rethink your motives. Sometime the best dishes take longer to cook. Be patient because you don't want to rush into marriage just for it to be a miserable experience. If your goal is to have the best wedding this world has ever seen, then you may want to rethink some things. Preparing for a wedding, which is one day and not preparing for the lifelong commitment may be a sign that you're not ready. Being married is about two people becoming one in a lifelong journey, not two people living separate lives in the same house. Selfishness is the root of every divorce. Carrying selfish desires into a marriage is the main ingredient for a recipe of disaster. If you are a selfish person when you are single, you will be a selfish person when you are married. There is not automatic switch that will make you unselfish once you say I do. You have to learn to be selfless before you actually get married. Fulfilling purpose and accomplishing a mission in a marriage is about two things. Partnership and the lives the partnership has as opportunity to impact. Those lives can be your children, family, friends or even people you may never meet. A mission is not about the people accomplishing the mission; it's about the people that will benefit from the mission once it's completed.

Married Couples

Many married couples have never considered what the mission is for their marriage. Couples sometimes get married and become comfortable and complacent. Your marriage life should not be about your comfort level; it should be about your impact level. Whether you have been

> *Being married is about two people becoming one in a lifelong journey, not two people living separate lives in the same house.*

married a long time or just said I do, discovering your mission can have invaluable results for the strength and longevity of your relationship. Having a mission minded marriage gives the couple a sense of purpose. Understanding purpose helps you define the "why" in your marriage. Knowing your "why" will lead you to your "what". What as a couple are you two designed to do together? Who will benefit when you accomplish your mission?

There is a formula that I use to direct people to purpose. Passion + Burden = Purpose

- Passion
  - That which you are good at doing
  - That which you love to do
  - Something you would do for free

- Burden
    - That which the world needs
    - That which burdens your heart
    - A problem in the world that you want to see fixed

If you were to take your passions as a couple and connect them with your burdens, I believe it will lead you to your purpose.

Jason Brown of Henderson, North Carolina played football for the University of North Carolina. In 2005, the Baltimore Ravens in the 4th round drafted Jason. At 6'3, 320 pounds Jason was a beast on the field. At one point in his career, he was the highest paid center in the NFL. In 2009, Jason signed a five-year, $37.5 million dollar contract with the St. Louis Rams. After earning $25 million of that contract, Jason Brown made a decision to walk away from the game of football. At the age of 29, Jason still had a lot of football left in him however, he felt something was greater for him in his life; he felt a greater purpose. Jason and his wife, Tay Brown started a farm called "First Fruits Farm." Jason saw the need of poverty and hunger in his region of North Carolina and decided to make a difference. The burden of children and families being hungry was greater than the contract and glory of the game of football. He and his wife felt they had a greater purpose in life and made it their mission to donate the first fruits of each harvest to local food banks in the North Carolina region. As a married couple, their mission was clear. When they understood their "why" they knew exactly "what" to do. They started a farm to impact the lives of hungry people in their community. Not many people would have walked away from such high paying game but Jason and his family understood why they were together. If you are married, here are a few questions I would like you to think about:

- What are you and your spouse's passions?
- What is a problem you want to see solved in the world?
- What are you guys good at?
- What is your burden?
- What is one thing you want to see changed in your community, city, state, etc.?

Thinking about these questions can help you and your spouse begin to understand what your purpose and mission can be in your marriage. It's not an overnight process, however starting the discussion can begin the journey to being a mission minded couple. Remember, fulfilling purpose is rarely about those accomplishing the purpose; it's about those that will benefit from the work that has been done. Steve Jobs accomplished his purpose and goal of creating the iPhone, but all iPhone users benefit from his work. Even though it's a rarity for purpose to be about those that accomplish it. In a marriage, there are benefits for couples when they pursue purpose together. Here are four benefits of having a mission in your marriage:

- Gives you a common goal
- Creates an environment where you work together
- Takes the focus off your problems in the marriage
- Opportunity to grow together

Common goal

Having a common goal in marriage is very important. Having a common goal in a marriage creates a team environment. Teammates have each other's back in a game. You don't focus on the mistakes or shortcomings of your teammate, you help them overcome them for the goal of winning the game. Remember, I said that having a mission would help you make certain decisions in your life. When you are working with a common goal in sight, things become clearer for you and your spouse. Let's say that your marriage mission is creating a business. Regardless of what type of business it is, you will have certain goals that will need to be accomplished for the mission. Your decisions will be shaped by your goals for the mission. Once you make a decision, your decisions will then make you. Everything you do will be centered on accomplishing the mission. As a couple you will now work together to achieve those goals. You will both use you skills, talents, and power to succeed. If your spouse falls short, that's where you come together and make up the difference for the sake of the team and the sake of the goal. In professional sports, the goal is to win a championship; in marriage you can have many goals but the main one should be staying together and loving each other as long as you both shall live.

Working Together

There is a biblical proverb that says, "Iron sharpens iron." This proverb is true in literal and metaphoric senses. People help other people to be sharp. There are approximately 4 million family owned businesses in the U.S., with

Once you make a decision, your decisions will then make you.

more than 1.4 million of those being run by a husband and wife team. Now I'm not saying you should quit your jobs and start a business together but I am saying that having a mission will pull you guys together and hopefully in the same direction. When couples first start dating, they often talk about their goals, visions and all the things they want to accomplish. As time passes and marriage comes into the picture and babies or jobs start happening, couples can loss that drive to dream. When we dream together it draws us closer. When we work on a common goal together it can sharpen us. No one knows you like your spouse, so no one will be able to help you become better than your life partner. View working together as building each other up; rather than breaking each other down.

Focus

Bills, babies, jobs, are just a few things couples can focus on. Just focusing on these things can be quite discouraging in a marriage. If all you do is focus on issues in your marriage then all you will see in your marriage is issues. Bills need to be paid. Babies need to be taken care of. Jobs need to be worked. However, where is the focus and attention on each other? Having a mission minded marriage can help you take the focus off your challenges and give you an opportunity to spend time together and channel that negative energy into a positive dream. I can remember early in my marriage, we

214

had an argument about something and were mad at each other. The day we were mad at each other was the same day we had tickets to go a comedy show. Not wanting to waste our money for tickets we had already purchased, we made the decision to go mad. The car ride to the show was silent and you could cut the tension in the air with a knife. When we got to the show, we didn't focus on

> *If all you do is focus on issues in your marriage then all you will see in your marriage is issues*

each other we just focused on having a good time and the show. While we were sitting there laughing we forgot what we were mad about and started enjoying each other's company. Focusing on having a good time was our mission. Laughing became our goal and what we were mad about didn't even matter anymore when focused on the mission and each other.

Growth

When a seed is planted in the ground, germination happens. Germination is the process in which a seed changes from a state of dormancy (just a seed) to a growing, living plant. A seed contains a tiny plant embryo as well as all of the nutrients an emerging plant needs to begin its growth cycle. In order for the plant's embryo to become a plant, key environmental factors must be present when the seed is planted. When a couple makes the decision to pursue a mission, they are making a decision to be planted with each other and grounded in their purpose. Over the course of pursuing purpose and accomplishing a mission in a marriage, there will be challenges along the way. Know that everything that is in you has prepared you for the journey ahead. Just as the seed has all the nutrients inside for it to be a plant; you have everything you need to be a mission minded couple. When a seed is planted, it will grow through the dirt and soil in order to be a plant. When you and your spouse make the decision to be planted in your mission you will grow through each obstacle, as long as you make the decision to do it together.

Chapter 19

Your greatest asset is each other

The most valuable asset is not a head full of knowledge. But a heart full of love with, and ear ready to listen and a hand willing to help.

Wise investors always look for a high return on their investments. This is also true in the matter of marriage, however many people want a return when they have not invested the time, resources, and energy into making a marriage great. After speaking with investors, many investors make the choice of long-term investments versus short-term investments. When you make an investment that you intend to keep for many years, you may be expecting the investment to increase in value so that you can eventually sell it for a profit. In a marriage, there is no selling for profit; it's the benefits and rewards along the way that make your investment worth it. When you purchase a short-term vehicle, you are generally not expecting much in the way of a return or an increase in value. That's why serial dating is such a waste of time. Why invest in a person that you don't plan to have a future with. When you think about it; many people waste years on people that will never marry them. Your spouse is not just a fling or brief interlude; this is your lifetime companion that will be with you in good and bad times.

Many spouses invest in so many other things rather than their mate. They invest in their job, cars, hobbies, schools, houses, clothes etc., the list could go on and on. Now these things are all good, but they can typically cost us more than the investment we make in them. So what am I saying; should you not have a career or hobbies? No, that's not what I am saying; I am saying that your spouse is your greatest asset, not the things you can accumulate. The cars, clothes and houses you invest in can never show up at your funeral, but the people you invest in will. Why not make a great investment in your spouse. There is 168 hours in a week. How much time would you say you invest in your spouse? I would like to break the investment down into three categories that would make it easier to understand. Time, Talk, and Touch are three areas of investment.

- Time – Time will be an interesting subject because all areas of investment will include time. Time is very important. It gives us a parameter of what is being done. How much time are you spending alone together? No kids, no outside distractions, just you two. If you could manage your time and found some time wasters of your day, would you invest that time in your spouse? The

  The cars, clothes and houses you invest in can never show up at your funeral, but the people you invest in will. Why not make a great investment in your spouse.

  time you invest in your spouse can have a major return and invaluable rewards for a couple. When you spend quality time with your spouse, you are saying that they are more important than the other things in your life.

- Talk – Once again time is involved because you have to ask yourself how much time do you and your spouse actually spend talking to one another. Not just talking about bills, the kids and all the challenges you may have. What about dreaming again? What about talking to each other and giving each other compliments? Telling your spouse how much they mean to you. Do you tell your partner that you value, appreciate and respect them? Communication in a marriage once again is the oil that keeps things flowing. No talk, no flow. One woman I interviewed for this book gave some wise advice for healthy communication in marriage. Her husband she cherished is now deceased. She told me that when she was married, she and her husband would turn off the television, put their child to sleep early so they would have time to have "pillow talk." Pillow talk is an awesome thing that a couple can do to remove all the distractions of the day and just connect. You make sure the kids are sleep. You turn off all the lights in your room. Turn the TV off. You lay on your back with your eyes to the ceiling or you can cuddle; however you like, it's up to you. You then just talk and share your heart with your mate. Share ideas, dreams, desires, etc. Whatever it is, invest that time to talk and connect with your mate.

- Touch – Now touch is not always about being intimately physical with your spouse. It involves activities, date nights, taking a walk etc. To touch someone you are in covenant with is to acknowledge their presence and to communicate your yearning for them. That's why the most successfully married couples believe that touching is an awesome experience and touching is a frequent occurrence. Dr. Charles & Elizabeth Schmitz have been researching married couples for over 30 years. For over three decades they have interviewed thousands of couples. What they have found to be a common trait in most successful marriages is the "accumulation of touching." They found that successful married couples hug, kiss, touch each other while they are talking, sitting on the sofa cheek to cheek while having conversations; cuddling around each other while in bed etc. These couples enjoy the intimate connection that touching brings and it adds value and appreciation for their spouse. Touching creates connection for moments to look forward to and remember.

I'm your ally not your enemy

World War II (WWII or WW2), was a global war that lasted from 1939 to 1945, though related conflicts began earlier. It involved the vast majority of the world's nations—including all of the great powers—eventually forming two opposing military alliances: the Allies and the Axis. It was the most widespread war in history, and directly involved more than 100 million people from over 30 countries. In a state of "total war," the major participants threw their entire economic, industrial, and scientific capabilities behind the war effort, erasing the distinction between civilian and military resources. Marked by mass deaths of civilians, including the Holocaust (in which approximately 11 million people were killed) and the strategic bombing of industrial and population centers (in which approximately one million were killed, and which included the atomic bombings of Hiroshima and Nagasaki), it resulted in an estimated 50 million to 85 million fatalities; this made World War II the deadliest conflict in human history. At the center of WW2 were Japan, Germany and Italy. The Empire of Japan aimed to dominate Asia and the Pacific and was already at war with the Republic of China in 1937, but the world war is generally said to have begun on September 1, 1939 with the invasion of Poland by Germany and subsequent declarations of war on Germany by France and the United Kingdom. From late 1939 to early 1941, in a series of campaigns and treaties, Germany conquered or controlled much of continental Europe, and formed the Axis alliance with Italy and Japan.

The attack on Pearl Harbor was a surprise military strike by the Imperial Japanese Navy against the United States naval base at Pearl Harbor in the United States Territory of Hawaii, on the morning of December 7, 1941. The attack led to the

United States' entry into World War II. The following day the United States declared war on Japan. Up until this attack, the United States was not heavily involved in WW2, but the attack proved that they could no longer just sit by and watch the world at war and do nothing about it. On January 1, 1942, the Allies of World War II were formed. This alliance was created to stop the axis, which included Germany, Japan and Italy military aggression over the world. There were other countries that supported the axis forces, however, these three were at the center of all aggression. The allies included 26 countries having one common enemy and one common goal; stopping the axis forces of Germany, Japan and Italy. The allied forces were at one time enemies and had been in wars against each other before but they realized that they had to put aside their differences in order to accomplish their goal and beat the enemy.

We can take a page from the history books and learn something from WW2. In marriage, we often create an enemy with our spouse. Outside pressures can make a couple turn against one another rather than turning to one another. Financial stress, children, illness', loyalty, jobs, In-laws, etc. In a marriage there could be a number of issues that could try to make your spouse the enemy but we must realize that our spouse is not our enemy, they are our allies.

223

When we make the choice to fight for each other and not with each other, we create a common goal and a common enemy. That common goal is creating a successful and disgustingly beautiful relationship that is healthy, growing and nurturing for both partners. The enemy is anything that will try to come between couples that were envisioned prior to exchanging your vows. It's certainly not an easy task, however, it's definitely worth it. Just like the allies of WW2, they had to come together and vow to defeat the enemy that was threating their world. As a married couple, you have to come together and vow not to let anything or anyone come between you and threaten your world. Respecting, honoring and loving each other in order to build that marriage that will stand the test of time and the test of challenges.

Piece by piece and battle after battle the Axis forces were defeated by the allied forces. In August of 1945, Japan finally surrendered. The Axis forces of Germany and Italy had already admitted defeat earlier that year and had exited the war. The Allied forces proved that persistence would beat resistance. They were able to put aside their previous wars and battles and became persistent about beating a resistant enemy.

Taking a look at your marriage, what enemies can you and your spouse come together to fight? You are each other's best asset and best ally in the fight for your marriage. Make the decision to fight for each other and not with each other.

Chapter 20

There is no room for automatic

Good things might come to those who wait. But the better things comes only to those who work hard to make it happen.

The year was 1982; I was the ripe age of 6, however, I was blessed with a great memory of my childhood. My dad was a man who loved Cadillacs. Like most little boys, I wanted to be just like my dad (which would explain my affinity for Cadillacs). 1982 was the year my dad purchased a Black Cadillac Eldorado. It was a 2 door car with leather seats and a wood oak panel for the dashboard. As a youngster, I would love when my father came home with a new car because he would always take me and my 2 siblings on a joy ride. My dad really liked to show off his cars. I remember this one time with this car in particular with which we took a trip to see my uncle. We lived in Miami, FL at the time and my uncle lived in St. Petersburg, FL, which was a 3-4 hour drive.

When we arrived in St. Petersburg, my dad went by my uncle's house to show off his latest purchase. I can remember sitting in the front seat between my father and uncle and my dad talking about the features of his new car. He showed him it's cassette player, which was a new technology for a vehicle at the time. He showed him the power seats and how they worked. But there was this one feature that really caught my attention while my dad was driving. It was the cruise control feature. This feature on the car allowed my dad to take his foot off the gas pedal and relax them if he had a long drive ahead of him. My dad would lean his seat back making it appear like the car was driving itself. I thought it was the coolest thing in the world and thought my dad was the smoothest man ever. When we were on the open highway and there was a long stretch of highway ahead of us, my dad would hit the button and it seemed like we would just coast along the highway with such ease. The car's technology was doing all the work and my dad was just along for the ride.

Now what does this have to do with being married? The truth is that many people once married think that they can just hit a button in their relationship and the relationship will just cruise along automatically with minimal effort and work. Some also think that being married is a switch that when you say "I Do," all the problems will be solved.

However, they have a rude awakening when they experience some challenges or issues in their relationship. Nothing in a marriage is automatic.. There is no cruise control button you can hit and just ride off into forever with your spouse. It's because of this mindset that many couples simply grow apart instead of growing together. Growing apart is dangerous and detrimental to a marriage. In my research for this book, I found 3 common things of couples that grow apart. Being bored in the relationship; living separate lives; and being stressed in the relationship. Now there are more than just 3 but I believe these are the most prevalent and habitual in marriages today.

> *Nothing in a marriage is automatic*

Being Bored

I interviewed several persons that were divorced or going through a divorce while preparing to write for this book. When I would ask the question "why are you getting a divorce" or "why are you divorced?" 70% said "we just grew apart." Daniel Jones of the Modern Love column for the New York Times was quoted as saying that marriage can also be boring punctuated with deadening routines, cyclical arguments and repetitive conversations. It's almost like watching the same movie over and over knowing all the

228

parts to the movie. You find yourself acting along in your favorite parts of the movie and not paying attention to a less interesting scene. Boredom is an indication that there is an absence of stimulation. If you're married, when was the last time you were stimulated in your marriage? What sparked that stimulation? Now I'm not just referring to physical stimulation. I'm also talking about the spiritual, emotional, mental, and social stimulation. If you don't want your marriage to be boring, then it's up to you to make it stimulating. Life is full of opportunities to learn and grow and expand our horizons and ourselves; we just need to take advantage of them. Read new books together, take a cooking or pottery class together, learn and share new ideas, invite over people outside your typical social circle, pursue a new mission in your marriage – all these things can bring more excitement and interest to your marriage. But, it won't happen if you do nothing you have to do something. No one is going to do it for you.

> *Boredom is an indication that there is an absence of stimulation*

If you're not married but you are aspiring to be married, knowing what stimulates you is key. If you are able to communicate that to your mate, it leaves the guessing work out and provides a better road map to achieve stimulation in your relationship. If you want a healthy stimulated relationship before you're married, it helps to be a stimulated person prior to marriage. I listened in on a counseling session of a married couple and the therapist said to the woman, "you're not bored, you're boring." Understanding that your partner will never satisfy 100 percent of your needs would help you not be disappointed if they were to fall short of some of your expectations. If you lived a boring life before marriage, don't expect you future spouse to come along and make things spark. You are two separate sparks that when you come together, you can make an explosion.

Living Separate lives

I consider Don and Caroline as my uncle and aunt. We are not related biologically but I have known them basically all my life. I grew up with all their children and we call ourselves cousins. Growing up, I paid close attention to Don and Caroline because I felt they had something unique. In 2015, Don and Caroline celebrated 47 years of marital bliss. I went to school with their sons Vincent, Donald, and Shannon. Shannon was just a year older than me, so he and I hung out with him more than the others but we were all family. I lived around the corner from them so in Jr. High, Shannon and I would walk to school together; and when

Shannon got a car in high school, I rode with him to school. Every morning when we were on our way to school, I saw Don and Caroline get in the same car and ride to work together. If I was there after school, Don and Caroline came home together as well. They both worked for the city in different departments and buildings but the two always rode together to work. If you saw Don, you saw Caroline. When we would go on summer vacations, these two would even wear matching and complementing outfits. They were so cute. As a youngster, I really didn't think about all the things they would do together but as an adult I look back and realize they have something really special. Both Don and Caroline made good money and could afford to get another car but they made the decision to have one car so they could ride together to and from work. When I talked to Shannon about his parents, he said that his parent had one car on purpose. They would say that if they had a disagreement they were forced to work it out in the car. They couldn't just go their separate ways, they had to work it out. I could only imagine the type of car rides they had. For over 20 years they shared the same car riding to work. Don and Caroline are both retired now. It wasn't until a few years ago that they got another car. However, I go to see them in Miami from time to time and it's still the same. They still wear matching outfits. The two are still inseparable. If you've seen Don, you've seen Carolyn. So what am I saying? Should you and your spouse only have one car? Should you guys wear matching outfits? No, that's not my point. My point is that Don and Carolyn made a decision not to live separate lives. They made the decision to live together and share the good, the bad and the ugly with each other. Of course there is nothing wrong with an evening out with the boys or spending time with just the girls; but the key is for you and your spouse not to live your lives separately. When this happens in a marriage, you take the risk of going and growing in different directions. Jobs, school, kids, friends and even family can try to pull you in a different or separate directions, but you need the time to meet in the middle and share the details of your day. You should never let a week go by without taking time out for each other. Maybe not an official date, but at least have pillow talk about each other without outside distractions. Growing apart is not imposed upon us by some mysterious outside vindictive force; we allow it to happen. We need to be proactive. If your spouse spends too much time on things outside your marriage, you need to bring it to their attention. You need to let them know if you feel neglected.

We must set aside regular time (daily time, date night) to check in. And you need to be engaged with what they are saying. I don't care if your wife is an Avon lady or your husband works in retail, ask about his or her day. Be interested in what they do. Share your joyful moments and your discouraging ones. You need to make the time to talk; it doesn't happen automatically.

Stressors in a Relationship

No one's life is without trials or challenges, some major and some minor. Some believe that buying a new house and or remodeling an old one is one of life's greatest stresses on a marriage. This calls for a reality check, reviving our perspective. If we are in this position, we are privileged and we should appreciate it and not fight with our spouse about the experience. One of the easiest things in the world is to snap at your mate during a pressurized situation.

The birth of a child can also prove to be a challenging experience and put pressure on a relationship. Not only is there a major emotional adjustment, but the wife she goes through a physical change. Not only are the demands on everyone's time so much greater but also both parents can get absolutely exhausted. A child can be one of the most stressful experiences but also the most rewarding. It's an unparalleled journey. It's important to be aware of this and try very hard not to say or do anything hurtful during this very sensitive time. Try to appreciate the blessing that has entered your lives and not add more pressure to an already stressful situation.

Unfortunately, sometimes stresses within life are not happy ones. Children can be seriously ill, they can face educational challenges or emotional challenges. They can have handicaps or learning disabilities. All of these issues can take a toll on a marriage. Many marriages have actually crashed and burned when dealing with an ill child. This would be the perfect time for unity and coming together, but many choose the opposite and turn away from each other and make the spouse the enemy
How does this happen? In certain cases, it could be that one spouse blames the other. In other instances, a spouse may blame himself or herself and go into a shell and not communicate. They may become depressed or even abusive. Looking at their spouse may remind them of the pain. It's easier to avoid contact than to constantly be vulnerable and hurting. When we go out together, all we think about is this trying situation, so we choose not to go out and we drift apart.

Spouses frequently have different coping skills. One may be very emotional. One may be more logical. One more be analytical and the other more of an free spirit. One wants to be hugged and one wants to search the internet for feasible solutions. Spouses can get frustrated by the behavior of their partner or by their lack of sympathy with their position. When we are frustrated, it is easy to be short-tempered with our husband or wife. The key is to recognize that this behavior can be attributed to the stress in our lives and is not really about the behavior in our spouse. This requires self-awareness and self-control, two traits in short supply under these trying circumstances.

Couples do grow apart, but it doesn't just happen. It is a choice, unknowing or not. And likewise, our choices and hard work can usually prevent this from happening.

Now all three of these behaviors take one thing to combat them. The enemy and solution of boredom, living separate lives and life stressors, is effort. When you make the choice to put in the effort, you are making the choice to have a better relationship. No relationship can survive on automatic, we have to put in the effort and work to have a thriving and disgustingly beautiful relationship.

Chapter 21

The Long Walk Home

Don't miss the beauty of the journey trying to get to the destination.

When I was in elementary school, I lived a 15-minute walk from school. However, it rarely took me 15 minutes to get home from school. It would take me much longer, sometimes an hour. Often I would stop to the candy house and get some candy. Many times I would stop by my friend's house before reaching home. I'd mess with a dog or just do anything, delaying the arrival to my house. My mom would often ask me why it took me so long to get home. As a boy, I wasn't concentrated on my destination I loved the journey. The journey of getting home created memories and experiences that I will never forget.

Likewise, intimacy within a marriage is not about the destination, it's about the journey. Intimacy shouldn't be rushed just to get to the end. It should be savored and enjoyed by creating memories and experiences that both you and your spouse can flashback to. When it comes to intercourse, there are two mindsets that are prevalent in marriage.

- Sex vs. Intimacy
- Quantity vs. Quality

For the sake of our conversation, sex would constitute as just having intercourse with no passion or connection. Going through the motions physically, but not connecting mentally, emotionally or spiritually. Intimacy involves connection on a deeper level. It's the mental, emotional and spiritual connection that a husband and wife share to strengthen their bond. Intimacy in the confines of marriage is special and requires affection, attention and attraction for your spouse and only for your spouse.

When it comes to quantity vs. quality, this can be a big debate among married couples. You may have a partner that is focused on how often you are intimate; while the other is focused on the intensity and passion level of each encounter. The key is not about who is right and who is wrong. It's about finding balance within your relationship. If both partners focus on satisfying the other, than no one loses and everyone is getting what they need. Satisfying your mate intimately takes communication. Intimacy goes beyond the bedroom. The best component for intimacy is how you communicate with your spouse. You cannot take it for granted that you will automatically know what they desire or require to reach their ultimate intimacy peak.

Men and women are different. One of the reasons for our differences is to bring balance. A man could be described as a microwave and a woman could be called a crockpot. When it comes to intercourse most men are like microwaves. All you have to do is punch a few buttons and ding they are ready. A wife may just simply touch her husband and he's ready to go. Meanwhile, most women on the other hand require more time to cook, like a crockpot. With a crockpot, the food takes its time to marinate. The spices are infused into the food and add more flavor to the meal the more it's cooked. Men think of it this way, have you ever tried to become intimate with your spouse and she turned you away saying that she didn't hear from you all day and now you want to come and touch me? What she is really saying is that she requires and desires your touch outside the bedroom. Stimulate her mentally, stroke her emotional and support her spiritually. Your wife wants to feel special, she needs you to be present in the moment with her, and she wants to feel appreciated. Remember intimacy is taking the long walk home. She may require a "good morning beautiful text" even if you just woke up next to her. Or maybe calls in the middle of the day to let her know you were thinking about her. This will make her feel special. Making her feel special is basically making her feel like she is the only women in the world and no one else exists. Pay attention when she talks to you and don't be engaged when she is telling you about her day. That's being present and in the moment with her. Value her time and make sure that when you are with her, you are present mentally. Don't be there physically and your mind is somewhere else. In this day and age, wives have a full plate. From working to school to being entrepreneurs all while still running a home and being our spouses. Supporting your wife and making her feel appreciated is key. She may be on a job that doesn't appreciate her. Your children may be too young to show that appreciation or they may be teenagers and have a lack of appreciation. Whatever it is, her husband should be her biggest foundation of support and appreciation. These are just a few things that could stroke her emotionally and show her that you care. You may say that your wife doesn't support you and that you need her support and appreciation. As her partner and leader of the family, you should display your leadership by example. You do it first. If there was a cork in a bucket and you wanted to make that cork float and rise to the top, you have to put water in the bucket first. The more water you put in the bucket the more the cork will float. The water goes in first and then the floating takes place. The same principle applies, if you want your wife to respond to you, fill her bucket first and watch her rise to the occasion of floating for you.

Wives, your husband may typically have a shorter attention span than you. Most men work in bullet points and highlights. That's why ESPN Sports Center is such an attention grabber for men. They give the highlights and move on to the next story. When it comes to intimacy, you must take time to understand your husband. Contrary to popular opinion, men do have mood swings and typically operate on a rhythm. It's important for wives to learn your husband's rhythm. You could ask your husband the same question at two different times and get two different answers based on his mood and the rhythm he may be in. Your husband's intimacy drive may be high and it may seem like he's always in the mood to be intimate. From a biological standpoint, testosterone is what pushes your husband. It's what gives him that great desire to want to be

physically intimate with you. The same way a women may be
hormonal during her time of the month is the same way a
man may desire physical stimulation. He can control it,
monitor it but mainly wants to be understood. Understand
that a husband wants and needs
to feel the physical desire from
his spouse. It makes him feel
special and wanted as well. The
road may be a little different but

Wives, you're his biggest cheerleader and no one should be rooting for him louder, stronger or more frequently than you

the destination is the same. Husbands and wives typically
want the same things but have a different method in getting
to the same destination. At the end of the day, a man wants
to be honored, respected and needs the approval of his
spouse. When your husband tries but fails, he still wants to
know you're proud of him. If he went for the promotion but
didn't get it, still let him know you're proud of him. Let him
know that regardless of what happens he's still the man of
your dreams. Your husband desires to be wanted by you.
Wives, you're his biggest cheerleader and no one should be
rooting for him louder, stronger or more frequently than
you.

My mom and dad were married at an early age. They were
just 20 & 21 when they got married. Like many married
couples in there 20's, they had a vibrant sex life and thus

produced 3 children to prove it. My dad died when I was eight years of age so I have found memories of him but we did not get a chance to spend a lot of time together. With my dad dying so young, my mom served as the lifeline for me to learn more about my father. I love talking to my mom because she would always share stories of her and my Dad and how they made things work in their marriage. I remember my mom was sharing with me how early in their marriage their intimacy life was way down. My mom was working at night and my dad was working long days. Energy levels were low, time was short and tempers were high. Seemed like all they had time for was to argue. He was frustrated because he felt she was avoiding her wifely duties. She felt neglected because he was not sensitive to her needs and plus my older brother was still a little guy and my sister was on the way. All these things put a strain on their marriage and their sex life. My mom said she had several heart to heart conversations with my dad for him to understand that she was more of a crockpot than a microwave. If she was tired, she wanted to know that he cared about her and the reason she was tired. He couldn't just come home and expect her to be ready just because he was ready. The intimacy was a process for her. Everything in her world was connected. If her mind was on the kids and all their needs, it was hard for her to be intimate. If the house was a mess then she wouldn't feel comfortable making love in a messed up house. He shared with her that all day he's at work with people that look up to him and think he's special but when he gets home, he doesn't get that same feeling. He wanted to feel honored when he got home as well. With sparing me the visual details, my mom said that their marriage made a great comeback in their intimacy level. I can remember being three years old; my dad coming home from work and giving my mom flowers. I saw this several times over the course of the 8 years that I spent with my father. My dad learned that he had to put in the work prior to the bedroom in order for the bedroom mood to take place. My dad and mom had a healthy thriving marriage up until his death. It wasn't easy but my mom said it was worth it.

> *Wives understand that your husband truly desires for you to desire him.*

Wives understand that your husband truly desires for you to desire him. His sex drive may be higher than yours but that may be one of his ways to express his love. There is no other time that a man is more emotional than after he is intimate. If that is a way for your husband to express his emotions then embrace it to connect with him. Don't reject him; connect with him. Husbands you must learn that the journey to having a marriage filled with passion and intimacy starts long before the bedroom. Next time you want to be intimate with your wife, take the long walk home; don't take any short cuts.

Chapter 22

Beyond the Body

Outer beauty may dim with time, but inner beauty grows with time

In every section of this book, I made a choice to address the issue of looking at your partner beyond the body. In marriage it is no different. This chapter will be short because the story I have is straight to the point and paints an awesome picture of what true love is when you look beyond the body.

Australian Model, Turia Pitt suffered burns to 65 percent of her body. She lost her fingers and a thumb on her right hand. She spent five months in a hospital after she was trapped by a grassfire in an ultra-marathon. Throughout this ordeal, the one constant thing Turia had was a then fiancé Michael Hoskins. Hoskins pledged to be by her side

no matter what. He quit his job and made the decision to be with her every step of the way during her recovery. It was a 5-year journey of recovery but the two finally married. They began telling their story and were interviewed by a CNN reporter. The reporter asked Michael the question: "Did you at any moment think about leaving her and hiring someone to take care of her so you could move on with your life?"
His reply touched the world:
"I married her soul, her character, and she's the only woman that will continue to fulfill my dreams."

Basically, he married her soul and character not her body. No one could ever foresee the tragedy this coupled faced but Michael made the decision to look beyond her body.

As time goes on in a marriage, your body may go through many changes but we all have to make the choice to look beyond the body and look at our spouse's soul and character.

Chapter 23

Building a Bridge

Pressure produces proof!!! A diamond is produced under pressure. Wine is   produced under pressure. Pearls are produced under pressure. If you are under pressure right now just know that the pressure you are experiencing will produce something. What you produce is up to you. Don't give up on your marriage it may be a diamond in the rough!

Some married couples do not like to admit it, but they have conflicts. Conflicts are actually common to all marriages. Most couples have their share of conflicts and some will admit that the disagreements have not been pretty good. Start with two selfish people with different backgrounds and personalities. Now add some bad habits and interesting idiosyncrasies, throw in a bunch of expectations, and then turn up the heat a little with the daily trials of life. Guess what? You are bound to have conflict. It's inevitable. Since every marriage has its tensions, it isn't a question of avoiding them but of how you deal with them. Conflict can lead to a process that develops togetherness or separation. You and your spouse must choose how you will act when conflict occurs. It's not a question of 'if', it's a question of 'when'.

When I was married, I had poor conflict resolution skills. I was very selfish in my marriage. I thought that I was always right and this proved to be very challenging. I was a self-centered person that didn't like to compromise. This left my marriage filled with conflict. One of my solutions when I would have conflict was to walk away; and no, that would not resolve anything. Another thing I did was the silent treatment. When I was married, we could go for days without having a civilized conversation. With no communication, few issues rarely got resolved. I lived my marriage like this for 8 years until I began to pay attention to my actions and how they were causing pain and suffering within my own home. There was a large gap between my ex-wife and me. I wanted to learn how to shorten that gap and bring us closer together. I learned that I had to build a bridge to bring us back together again.

One reason we have conflict in marriage is that opposites

attract. Usually a task-oriented person marries someone who is more people-oriented. People who move through life at rapid speeds seem to end up with spouses who are slower-paced. It's strange, but that's part of the reason why you married who you did. Your spouse added a variety, zest, and difference to your life that it didn't have before.

> *Your differences are to bring balance not separation.*

But after being married for a while (sometimes a short while), what attracted you before becomes the thing that gets on your nerves. You may argue over small irritations such as how to squeeze a tube of toothpaste or over major ethical differences in handling finances or raising children. You may find that your backgrounds and your personalities are so different that you wonder how and why you two got together in the first place.

It's important to understand these differences, and then to accept and adjust to them. Your differences are to bring balance not separation. I want to share 5 things that can help build a bridge for you and your spouse to resolve conflicts.

Confront

You can never conquer what you refuse to confront. All of our differences are enlarged in marriage because they feed what is undoubtedly the biggest source of our conflict; our selfish nature. Maintaining harmony in matrimony has been difficult since the beginning of time. Ever since Adam and Eve (husbands and wives) have had two opinions about the situations they were in, two people being married together and trying to go their own selfish, separate ways could no longer hope to experience the oneness of marriage that it was designed to bring. We are all self-centered, we all instinctively

> *You can never conquer what you refuse to confront*

look out for number one, and this leads directly to conflict. Marriage offers a tremendous opportunity to do something about our selfishness. To experience oneness, you must give up your will for the will of another. Pursuing resolution of a conflict means setting aside your own hurt, anger, and bitterness for the sake of the team and partnership. There is nothing wrong with confronting your spouse about an issue if your goal is to resolve the issue and not just argue. Confronting your spouse with kindness and tactfulness requires wisdom, patience, and humility. Here are a few other tips I found useful to help confront your spouse about issues you may be facing.

- Check your motivation. Will your words help or hurt? Will bringing this up cause healing, wholeness, and oneness, or further isolation?

250

- Check your attitude. Loving confrontation says, "I care about you. I respect you and I want you to respect me. I want to know how you feel." Don't hop on your bulldozer and run your spouse down. Approach your spouse lovingly.

- Check the circumstances. This includes timing, location, and setting. Don't confront your spouse, for example, when he or she is tired from a hard day's work, or in the middle of settling a squabble between the children. Also, never criticize, make fun of, or argue with your spouse in public.

- Check to see what other pressures may be present. Be sensitive to where your spouse is coming from. What's the context of your spouse's life right now?

- Listen to your spouse. Seek to understand his or her view, and ask questions to clarify viewpoints.

251

Be sure you are ready to take it as well as dish it out. You may start to give your spouse some 'friendly advice' and soon learn that what you are saying is not really their problem, but yours!

Compartmentalize

During your time of confrontation, stick to one issue at a time. Don't bring up several. Don't save up a series of complaints and let your spouse have them all at once. This is dangerous and will be overwhelming to your partner. I hear husbands accuse wives of this often. Wives can sometimes hold on to a few issues and decide to bring them up all at once. If this is your method of dealing with issues, this can push your partner away rather than drawing them closer. The idea to resolving conflict is to bring closure and move forward from the situation. When I worked in corporate America, we had staff meetings. Every once in a while, a meeting would require us to address issues where someone may have dropped the ball. In these meetings, we would address the issues and say things like "Ok, going forward, how will this be handled." Or we would put a check and balance system in place in order to alleviate any issues addressed. It was important for us to compartmentalize the issues and not lump everything into one big problem.

If there is a pattern of behavior that keeps reoccurring then this is something different. Even in a behavioral pattern, it's important to be sensitive to the issue. Still address the pattern from a place of resolve and moving forward. Stay away from words like "you always" and "you never." Some behavioral patterns may require professional assistance from a licensed therapist or counselor. The key is staying on task and not making a gumbo of all the issues of your relationship in one setting. Address one issue at a time and stay focused on the resolution.

Commitment

There is a difference between interest and commitment. If you are interested in resolving a conflict in your marriage, you do what is convenient. When you are committed to resolving conflict in your marriage, you accept no excuses only results. In a marriage, you have to be committed to resolving the issues you have and not just playing the blame game. Focus on the problem, rather than the person. For example, you need a budget and your spouse may be reckless in their spending. Work through the plans for finances and make the lack of budget the enemy, not your spouse. Concentrate on conduct rather than character. This is the "you" message versus the "I" message again. You can assassinate your spouse's character and stab them right to the heart with "you" messages like, "You're always late; you don't care about me at all; you don't care about anyone but yourself." The "I" message would say, "I feel frustrated when you don't let me know you'll be late. I would appreciate if you would call so we can make other plans." This is a good way to convey your feelings without personally attacking your spouse. Pay attention on the facts rather than judging motives. If your spouse forgets to make an important call, deal with the consequences of what you both have to do next rather than say, "You're so careless; you just do things to irritate me."

Above all, stay focused on understanding your spouse rather than on who is winning or losing. When your spouse confronts you, listen carefully to what is said and what isn't said. For example, it may be that they are upset about something that happened at work and you're getting nothing more than the brunt of that pressure. When you are committed to resolving your conflicts, your focus is on results not excuses. As a married couple, your focus is resolving conflict and staying together, not staying mad at each other.

Communication

Every marriage operates on either the "Insult for Insult" or the "Grace for Insult" relationship. Husbands and wives can become extremely proficient at trading insults about the way he looks, the way she cooks, or the way he drives and the way she cleans house. Many couples don't seem to know any other way to relate to each other. Many times it's not what you say but the way you say it.

What does it mean to return a grace for an insult?

To be gracious first means stepping aside or simply refusing to retaliate if your spouse gets angry. Changing your natural tendency to lash out, fight back, or tell your spouse off is just about as easy as changing the course of the Mississippi River. However, the Mississippi River has changed its course under the right conditions. In this case those conditions would be how you communicate with one another.

It also means doing good. Sometimes doing good simply takes a few words spoken gently and kindly, or perhaps a touch, a hug, or a pat on the shoulder. It might mean making a special effort to please your spouse by performing a special act of kindness. Communication is more than words; it's also in your actions. Being gracious means seeking peace, actually pursuing it. When you eagerly seek to forgive, you

255

are pursuing oneness, not isolation. Your communication in your marriage has to be HOT. Honest, Open and Two-way.

Compromise

Compromise can be a bad word in many relationships. Compromise doesn't mean you're wrong and the other person is right. It means that you value your relationship much more than your ego or agenda. No matter how hard two people try to love and please each other, they will fail. With failure comes hurt. And the ultimate relief for hurt is the soothing salve of forgiveness and compromise. The key to maintaining an open, intimate, and happy marriage is to ask for and grant forgiveness quickly and compromise often. The best thing in marriage is to learn the habit of compromise. It is better to bend a little than to break a relationship.

Forgiving means giving up resentment and the desire to punish. By an act of your will, you let the other person off the hook. There is no love without forgiveness and no forgiveness without love.

One of the couples I interview for this book was married for 54 years. When I asked them what was one of the keys to a good marriage is, they told me that they could not just give me one thing but they would have to give me two. I gave my full attention to hear what they had to say. The husband leaned in close and told me to forgive and compromise. He said nothing is unbearable when you choose to forgive. You have to view forgiveness as a black card. A black card has no limit and can pay for anything. When you have that mentality, there is nothing you can't accomplish within your marriage. Once you make up in your mind that your partner will make mistakes and will do things that are wrong, it's easier to forgive. As we were talking, the wife interjected her feelings and said that compromise was the oil in their relationship. It kept things moving. Compromise isn't about winning and losing a battle. Remember you're on the same team so there is no need to fight. Just compromise and the team will always win in the end.

Resolving conflict in a marriage is a learned skill. I had to learn the hard way and from my mistakes in my first marriage. There is a saying that says "You win some and you lose some." Looking back over my marriage, I had to change it just a little. "You win some and you learn from some." I didn't lose, I actually learned something. I made the choice to be better and not bitter; to move forward and not stay stuck in my past. It was a painful but valuable lesson. What I learned shaped and molded me into the man I am today.

I'm stronger, I'm wiser, and I have learned what it means to have a Disgustingly Beautiful relationship.